A SWIPE IN THE
WRONG
DIRECTION

a Novella by
CARLOS HARLEAUX

Published by 7th Sign Publishing

peauxeticexpressions.com

Book Cover Design by Element Rose

Photography by Chris Booth

Copyright ©2020 by Carlos Harleaux

ISBN - 13: 978-0-578-72252-8 (Swipe Left Edition)

ISBN - 13: 978-0-578-72255-9 (Swipe Right Edition)

Printed in the United States

Harleaux, Carlos

A Swipe in the Wrong Direction

All rights reserved. No part of this book may be reproduced or transmitted in any form or by any means without written permission from the author/ and or publisher.

CHAPTER 1

"Candy? Hey, you finally answered. I have been trying to get in contact with you for a while. Um, how have you been?" Mike asked.

"The hostility doesn't let up. I'm better. How are you? I'm sorry for being MIA. I had to take some time to get myself together. I was headed down a bad road," Cookie explained. Despite a few touch-and-go check-ins, Cookie had not had an in-depth conversation with Mike in nearly a year.

Mike knew she was still healing from Ken's death and didn't want to push her. He knew she needed to grieve and recover in her own time.

"It's ok. I'm honestly giving you a hard time. I'm glad to hear from you. What's new?" he asked.

"Oh, you know, taking care of Breanna and taking it one step at a time. Mike, I owe you an apology," Cookie paused.

"Ok, thanks, I guess. I don't think you do. For what?" he inquired.

"Yes, let me explain. I know I told you I was going away

for a little while to regroup. That was a lie. I hate to admit it, but I had become an alcoholic, Mike. You didn't deserve to be around me like that, even as a friend," Cookie continued.

Even as a friend? Mike thought.

Was she implying they could have been more than friends? He didn't interrupt and let her finish her statement, without reading too far between the lines.

"I'm so embarrassed. I can't believe I told you that, but I had to get it off my chest. We have been through a lot," she exhaled, relieved to confide in her old friend.

"Cookie, don't you feel embarrassed for one bit. I'm proud of you. I had no idea all that was going on. Regardless, you've done something not many women or people period have the courage to do. You're still an amazing woman and a wonderful mother. Don't ever doubt that," Mike reassured her.

He felt a dull pang tug at his heart. The thought of Cookie going through such an ordeal made him feel sick. Mike only wanted great things for her. He was glad to hear her take ownership of her actions to make a better life for her and her daughter, Breanna.

"Mike, you have not changed after all these years. Why can't all men be like you? You are so loyal. Enough of my sad sap stories. Life is turning around for me now. God has spared me for some reason, so I have to give Him thanks and show that I'm grateful for another chance," Cookie stated.

"That's great to hear. God has smiled on you, Candy. I wouldn't exactly say all men should be like me, but I appreciate the vote of confidence," Mike chuckled.

"Hey, I'm telling the truth. These guys out here are pathetic. I tried to get back out there on the dating scene, but it required too much effort. So many of these men are losers. I know the ladies are all over you now that you're free and single. Any new dating escapades on your end?" Cookie inquired.

Mike wasn't sure of her tone. She didn't seem to be asking for her own personal interest, but more so from the perspective of a concerned friend. Cookie was a wild card though, so he was never too sure of her intentions.

"My dating life is pretty lame. Work has been keeping me ridiculously busy," he replied.

"Come on now. All work and no play will drive anyone crazy," she interrupted.

"I'm serious. None of these women out here are worth investing my time in. I've had my share of fun here and there, but nothing serious," he concluded.

Mike had to save face and make it seem like his love life was more eventful than it had been.

"Well, I understand that. Maybe you should try one of those online dating apps. I haven't had success with it, but I'm sure it's probably different for men. Everyone has a representative and it's all peaches and cream until their true colors start showing," she sighed.

"Online dating? Wait. You tried that? I never would have thought in a million years that you would try online dating," he laughed.

"I know, right. I can check it off my list now to say I've done it. Been there, got the t-shirt and only use it to work out in," she snickered.

Mike responded with a guttural laugh. An awkward silence filled a small gap in their dialogue.

"I can't say I'll be joining you on the online dating journey. Some of my friends have encouraged me to try online dating. Hell, even my mom has been pressuring me. She thinks it's been way too long since I've had a serious relationship. You'd think it wouldn't be this hard to pick 'em in your mid-thirties, right?" Mike replied.

"Exactly. We should be seasoned daters by now. What are we gonna do?" Cookie laughed.

Mike felt a lump form in his throat. Everyone thought he wasn't dating because he was still heartbroken about his failed engagement. However, that wasn't totally the case. He was still in love with Cookie, even after so many years. Maybe this was his chance to try again. His feelings for her were relentless and he didn't want to give up on the one woman he genuinely loved.

"Hey, you know…. I've been thinking. I know you're working through some things. I'm working through some things. How about I take you and Breanna out for some ice cream this weekend?" he asked.

Mike felt like a weight of bricks had been lifted from his shoulders. He clenched his teeth in anxious silence, awaiting her response.

"Mike, that sounds awesome. Let's play it by ear. I'm so careful now. I mean, of course I know you, but I need to watch out for Breanna's best interest. Plus, I don't know if I'm fully ready to get back out there and seriously date anyone. You are so sweet though," Cookie let him down gently.

"No worries. You can't blame a man for trying, right?" Mike replied nonchalantly.

Mike knew "let's play it by ear" was Cookie's nice way of saying, "It's not gonna happen".

He was tired of waiting for her to see his value after all these years. There was only one thing left to do. Mike decided he would have meaningless, random sex with whatever women he wanted. There would be no strings attached and he would live in the moment.

CHAPTER 2

"Hello?" Mike answered. "Man, I'm almost ready. Give me five more minutes and I'll be right out."

"Man, you always say that. Five minutes for you is like twenty. You're worse than a woman. You better be glad it's your birthday," Tavin responded.

Mike could hear ice crunching in a glass in the background. Tavin must have been preparing another cocktail.

"Whatever. You make sure Ben is ready. He's usually later than me," Mike replied, laughing as he put his friend on speaker phone to finish getting dressed.

"It's a new day. We're both waiting on you, chump," Ben replied.

"Well, this is a first. Ok, I'm leaving the room now. Are we meeting downstairs in the lobby?" Mike asked.

They all gathered for his 35th birthday and his best friends decided he needed to do something big to celebrate. Ben and Tavin felt he needed to live his best life now that he was a single man again. He didn't think turning 35 warranted a trip. Apparently, his friends thought otherwise.

All three men had distinctly unique personalities, but they clicked well together. Mike considered Ben and Tavin his brothers.

"No, come to Ben's room. I'm already here," Tavin replied.

"Ok, be there in a sec," Mike said. Ben's room was down the hall and around the corner.

They had no issue staying in the same room in their college days. However, now that they were all older, they preferred having their own space. Plus, they all wanted the liberty to invite a woman back to their room in privacy. Ben had already indulged in a one night stand the evening prior.

Mike arrived at room 725 and knocked on the door.

"Look who decided to join their own party?"

Tavin gasped as he swung open the door.

"Must be the birthday boy. We are getting wasted tonight," Ben said, immediately going in on all the places they would somehow end up visitig before sunrise.

"Yep, and this is for you man," Tavin said, handing him a $100 bill. "Use this wisely. You know, only on women, gambling, and booze," he laughed.

"Well, thank you, Tavin. Greatly appreciated," Mike laughed heartily.

"I paid for your plane ticket. I'm buying all your drinks tonight, so the booze part is on me," Ben replied.

"Seriously, I'm grateful to get away for a bit. I must admit, this was a great idea. Wait. Should I sit on this bed?" Mike joked before he eased down on the corner of the foot of the bed.

"Oh, yeah. The bed is safe. Tavin, I should have warned you about that chair you're sitting in.... Oh well," Ben chuckled.

"Goodness. I knew I had a funny feeling about that chair before I sat down," Tavin said, as he stood up quickly.

"Come on, let's go," Ben rebutted.

They all moved towards the door and checked to ensure they had their respective room keys.

"So, what's the move for tonight Ben?" Tavin asked. Although Ben was the youngest of the three (31 years old), he liked to feel like he was in charge. Tavin and Mike decided to avoid the senseless banter and let him feel like he was bossing them around.

"Let's say this will be a birthday Mike never forgets," Ben laughed, as he patted Mike on the shoulder.

As the elevator door opened, they spilled out, welcomed by Bruno Mars's blaring "24K Magic". Ben led the way towards the blackjack table. Tavin and Mike followed closely behind.

They played a few rounds of blackjack. Tavin never played before and enjoyed some beginner's luck. Meanwhile, Ben handed Mike a glass of Grey Goose and Sprite. Mike didn't notice, at first, because he was intently enthralled with his phone.

"Here, this is to get you started. There will be plenty more where this came from," Ben smiled.

"Ah, ok. Thanks man. I appreciate it," Mike replied, with his left hand extended to take the drink. He was texting vigorously with his right hand and staring down at his phone.

"Dude, that better not be Kelly," Ben said, shaking his head.

"Yeah man. She was wishing me a happy birthday, that's all," Mike said, nonchalantly.

"Ok, well it doesn't take that many keystrokes to say,

'thank you' and press 'send'," Ben rebutted.

"You know, as much as I hate to admit it, he's got a point, Mike. You know you and Kelly aren't getting back together. She's playing mind tricks on you. She cheated and you were completely faithful. Let her go," Tavin chimed in.

"Unless you have something to tell us. It's ok if you had your fun too, Mike. Hey, I'd say you deserved it, if you did. Tit for tat and more tits, right?" Ben joked.

"There is no tit for tat. All of this is still fresh, you know," Mike said, as he glanced upward, expecting empathy from his friends.

"Fresh? Your breakup with Kelly was well over a year ago. Wake up. It's over…. shit. I didn't know it was possible to lose my buzz before I got one," Ben ranted.

"Ben, take it easy on the birthday boy. We're going to get your mind off her, Mike, at least for tonight. I don't know about you two, but I'm hungry," Tavin interjected, as he tried to keep the peace.

"I am too. Yes, let's eat. How about Raku? I want to try that place," Mike said.

Although he wasn't fond of Ben's delivery, he knew his friend was right. Him and Kelly were engaged and together almost three years. He felt like it was going to take at least that same amount of time to fully get over her. Honestly, he was excited she even thought to text him on his birthday.

"Awesome. It's your pick. Sounds good to me," Ben replied.

"Yep, me too," Tavin said. "I think it's about half a mile from here. Should we walk it?"

"The weather is nice out tonight. Yeah, let's go for it," Mike said.

They made their way to the restaurant, reminiscing

on old stories from their college days and how immature they were back then. All three men were successful now. Ben was a marketing manager (and in the running for a hefty promotion soon), Tavin was the regional director for a booming new beverage company and Mike recently landed a VP role at a thriving music streaming company.

Mike, Tavin, and Ben all loved the food, the service, and the atmosphere at Raku. Apparently, they were right on time because the ambiance was turning into a dance vibe, which was perfect for Mike's birthday. Tavin stepped away from the table, midway through their dinner to go take a call. Moments later, after he returned, the staff snuck up behind Mike with a flaming desert that had colorful, twisted candles sprouting out of it.

The staff sang 'Happy Birthday' to Mike as they placed the generous slice of pecan caramel cheesecake on the table. The pounding bass of Justin Timberlake's "Sexy Back" nearly drowned out their voices. Mike took a few bites of the desert, as Tavin and Ben split the collective dinner tab.

"Well, you heard the man. Get out there and show 'em you still got it," Tavin joked, as they made their way to the dance floor.

Meanwhile, Ben scouted out a beautiful woman for Mike to dance with. His friend had no problem picking up women, but he wanted to help him get out of his breakup funk as quickly as possible.

Tavin was already on the dance floor with a woman he spotted earlier when they entered Raku. He was the most charismatic out of all three guys. He usually attracted gold diggers. So, he decided to have fun and only get into a serious relationship if it fell in his lap. Meanwhile, he was fine with…. well, whatever fell in his lap.

Soon, they all were in their own world, as they tossed back drinks, danced with random beautiful women, and repeated that cycle well after midnight.

"Whew, I haven't done anything like that in years. I'm on top of the world right now. Yeah!" Mike yelled, as they exited the restaurant and stepped onto the main strip.

"Mission accomplished?" Ben asked, as he nudged Tavin. He kept a watchful eye on Mike, who was noticeably tipsy.

"Yep, I'd say so and the night is still young," Tavin replied, as he gave Ben a high five.

CHAPTER 3

"You know, I never thought I would say this, but I'm actually worn out," Ben said.

"Yeah, I'm with you on that man. Wow, it is 3:45 am. Maybe that's why," Tavin replied, as they all laughed.

"I don't know what it is, but I still feel like I'm bouncing off the walls," Mike said.

"Damn, did somebody put a roofie in this guy's drink? I thought we would be dragging him to stay awake by now," Tavin whispered to Ben.

"I know, right. I was thinking the same thing," Ben replied.

They entered the main entrance of the hotel, but Mike barely even recognized where they were. Surprisingly, he was still able to stroll without much wavering.

"Well, I'm glad you're bouncing off the walls. You should be and the night still isn't over for you," Ben said.

They got on the elevator and Tavin pressed the button for the seventh floor. A young group of twentysomethings got off on the second floor before them.

"Well man, let's go ahead and go up to your room for a bit," Tavin added.

"Alright, that's cool with me," Mike said. Mike unlocked the door, but his key didn't work. He kept trying but a red light appeared above the handle. "Ugh, I guess I need to get my card rekeyed. I'll be right back," he said.

"Wait, man. Isn't your room number 736?" Ben asked.

"Ha! This is 728. 736 coming right up. Just a few more steps," Mike joked, as they all lazily marched toward to his correct room. He unlocked the door and flipped on the light switch. Ben stretched out in the middle of the bed.

"Hell, should I even lay here? Is it safe?" he joked.

"Hmm, well it might not be after tonight," Tavin replied, as he moved towards the door. A soft knock followed. "Oh my, who could this be?" he said, in a dramatic tone.

While Tavin answered the door, Ben turned on some music from Mike's portable Bose speaker.

"Jackpot. A little ambiance. Good evening ladies. Or should I say, rise and shine?" he smiled, as two scantily clad twin bombshells sauntered through the door.

They were nearly identical, except for their haircuts (one had an asymmetrical, short blonde bob and the other had flowing auburn shoulder length hair, with golden highlights). Mike's mouth hung open as his eyes zoomed in on their full, perky breasts, flawlessly smooth olive toned skin and thickly shaped legs.

"Hmmm, are you the lucky birthday man?" The one with the bob haircut whispered in Mike's ear.

"Let's get you off this bed and onto the chair. You've been a bad boy and it's time to be spanked", the other twin said, as she put the heel of her boot right between Mike's legs in the chair.

Her crotch was strategically placed right in front of his mouth. Mike moved his head closer to connect his lips with the inside of her thighs.

"Whoa, slow down soldier," Tavin laughed. Ben gave the ladies some cash and then announced that he and Tavin were about to leave.

"I can't believe you guys are about to miss out on all the fun. You'd be crazy to leave right now," Mike sighed, with his attention still focused on the twins.

"You will be fine without him," Tavin joked.

He left two condoms on the dresser before he exited the room with Ben.

"We'll make sure to take good care of him," Both of the twins said in unison.

Ben observed and rubbed his hands together as he gestured to Mike with a look that said, "get 'em tiger".

"Man, do you think it was a bad idea for us to leave?" Ben asked.

"Was it a bad idea? Hell yeah, it was a bad idea. We're good friends though, so good karma is on its way to us," Tavin said.

"I guess you've got a good point. Besides, he won't miss us one bit," Ben said, as they continued towards the elevator.

"Nope. Oh yeah and I have his phone too. So, Kelly won't have any chance to disturb his groove," Tavin laughed. He tapped Mike's phone against his palm.

"What the hell? You stole his phone? Geesh… I'm supposed to be the crazy one," Ben replied and shook his head in disbelief.

"I didn't exactly steal it. I saw that he was about to leave it in the restroom at the restaurant. I've been holding on to it ever since. I conveniently forgot to give it back to him,"

Tavin laughed.

"Man, you are a trip," Ben replied.

"Hey, wait a sec. Before you go to your room. I need your help. Let's set up Mike on one of those dating apps. I know you've been on a few. I can't sit by and keep letting him waste his life behind Kelly. I know you've got to be tired of it too," Tavin suggested.

"This keeps getting better. Your idea might be crazy enough to work. If he meets a good woman on the app, it might turn things around for him. Hell, if he doesn't, he can at least have some fun in the meantime," Ben agreed.

"My thoughts exactly. Hmmm…. this one appears enticing. Have you heard of 'Sweet Nothings'?" Tavin inquired.

"Oh yeah, I had a few memorable nights because of that app," Ben answered, with a wide-mouthed grin.

Tavin handed Mike's phone to Ben. Within a few minutes, Ben set up Mike's profile, with specific preferences.

"Done. Now, we wait for the ladies to come to him. This is going to be good," Ben snickered.

CHAPTER 4

"Ugh, goodness," Mike groaned as the sunlight peered through the thin slit in the curtains.

He tried to sit up in the bed, but his head felt too heavy. Mike glanced over at the clock. 8:03 am. He assumed he had only slept a couple of hours. The evidence from last night's escapade was strewn across the room.

There was an opened condom wrapper near his head on the pillow. Two empty bottles of champagne were on the nightstand. His underwear hung off the corner of the handle. His pants and shirt were off. A faint scent of some type of vanilla and berry scented fragrance rested on his upper lip.

Boom. Boom. Boom.

His head spun violently inside. He had to be dreaming. Mike could hear voices on the other side of the door yelling, "Open up. Rise and shine." He squinted at the clock again. 9:54 am. Great. He hoped it was closer to Noon. Mike forced himself out of bed, threw some shorts on, and answered the door.

"Aren't you guys supposed to be still sleeping? We

didn't get back here until right before 4:00 am this morning," Mike complained.

"So what? It's your birthday celebration. Suck it up. We've got more partying to do, and there's nothing you can do about it. Oh, but you're paying for yourself today," Ben laughed.

"Pretty much what he said. Here's your phone back," Tavin said, as he tossed the phone in Mike's direction. "You may want to check your messages. I think your mom called you. She's checking up on her baby. Are you going to tell her all about the twins and their twins?" he continued, with a raised eyebrow.

"I'll call her back later," Mike replied.

He still felt a bit dazed and bewildered.

"Yep, this is all you bud. Somebody had an exciting night. We did a great job," Ben said, as he examined the entire room.

"We want to hear all about it. Clean yourself up, get dressed and we'll be waiting for you down at the lobby so we can get some breakfast. 10:30 am good?" Tavin asked.

"Sure, that will work. Alright, I'll see you two in a bit then," Mike responded.

He plugged his phone on the charger and brushed his teeth. Although he felt sluggish from partying into the early morning, it was the best time he had in a while.

He heard several alerts go off on his phone when he was in the shower. Some of the alerts sounded unrecognizable but he chalked it up to his hangover. A low-pitched gong that sounded like it should be in Benihana. He must have accidentally reprogrammed something last night.

10:25 am. Mike put on his shoes and traveled toward the elevator to meet Ben and Tavin downstairs. He grabbed his phone and sprayed a few squirts of his favorite cologne;

an old birthday gift that Kelly got him a couple years ago. It was nearly all gone now.

He called his mom on the way downstairs after listening to her voicemail. She called him to see how his birthday celebration was going.

"Hello? Is this my birthday man? 35 years ago, to the day. Wow, time really does fly," she said. He could hear her smile through the phone.

"Hey Mom, it's been a great time. Tavin and Ben didn't let me get much sleep. I'm still recovering this morning and about to go down to meet them for breakfast," he laughed.

"Did you meet any nice ladies there?" She asked. Mike knew where this was going.

"Well, Las Vegas isn't exactly the place for that mom, but I've been keeping my eyes open," he obliged her. He wasn't about to let on that he had ménage à trois with two strippers that he couldn't remember by name in his drunken stupor.

"Ok then, well I'm sure it's been a great time. You know, it's been so long since Kelly. It's time to move on. I don't want you to be lonely," she said, in a concerned tone.

"Well, I never said I was lonely mom. I promise, I'm good," he assured her. "I'm downstairs now to meet the guys in the lobby, but I'll call you when I get back in town. I love you."

"I love you too. Don't get into too much trouble out there and enjoy the rest of your trip," she said.

Tavin and Ben were enthralled in a conversation when Mike turned the corner.

"Hey, there he is. We figured we would catch the tail end of the breakfast here the hotel since you had such a long night," Ben joked.

"Yeah man, those twins were amazing. The way they

moved their..." Mike explained, before he was cut off by Tavin.

"Hey, save the details for yourself. We're jealous because we didn't stay. No, I'm joking. I want every freaky, nasty detail. I'm all ears," Tavin laughed.

They eventually made their way into the breakfast area and discussed the nitty gritty about last night. The waitress came by to take their orders, but they hadn't even checked out the menu yet.

"Good morning, guys. I can give you another moment to select your menu options. Our breakfast will end in about 45 minutes," the waitress said.

"I promise, we'll have it together in the next five minutes," Tavin replied, with a genuine smile.

"Wait a minute. What are all these messages on my phone and where did this app come from?"

Mike mumbled as the waitress marched away. Ben quickly shot a glance at Tavin and returned his gaze back to the menu.

"You're were going to find out sooner or later, but I may as well come clean now. I did it. I put the dating app on your phone last night. You have to shake this pathetic hold on Kelly. For Christ's sake, you're still wearing that cologne she bought you two years ago. If you want her back, go get her. Personally, I think there's no better way for you to get over her than seeing, or screwing, other women. Keep it casual. No strings. Have some fun for a change," Tavin ranted.

"Wow, you are crazier than I thought. I can't believe you would do something so stupid. I don't have a problem getting with a woman. I'm single by choice. You two should try it sometimes. You knew about this too?" Mike gestured to Ben.

A SWIPE IN THE WRONG DIRECTION

"Um, yeah I was there when he set it up," Ben admitted.

"Well, let's at least see who's hit you up already," Tavin exclaimed, to diffuse the situation.

"You're lucky you paid for this trip. I hate you both," Mike said, with an approving expression as he perused the photos.

"Let us see too. You might need some better judgment," Ben joked.

Mike leaned forward and placed his phone on the table so all of them could see the screen. "Ok, she looks good. A little nerdy, but in a naughty schoolteacher sort of way. Guess I'll swipe left to keep her."

"Dude, you deleted her. She wasn't too big of a loss though. Remember, swipe right if you're interested and left for the hell no's," Tavin informed him.

They collectively went through a few more profiles. Mike swiped right for a couple of ladies and swiped left for most of them. They stopped for a minute to order their food and then continued the search. That's when they saw her. Her screen name was LisaLuck. Almond shaped eyes. Full lips. Gorgeous smile. Voluptuous curves with a taught, petite frame. 31 years old.

"Damn boy, if you don't wanna get lucky with that, I will," Ben said.

"Umph, you can say that again. She's a keeper man," Tavin added.

"Yeah, she's the best one yet," Mike agreed, as he eagerly swiped left.

"Don't put all your C cups in one basket. There will be plenty more LisaLucks to come and give her a run for her money. Keep her at the top of the list," Ben advised.

CHAPTER 5

2:14 am. Mike laid in bed, restless. The room was completely silent and only the sound of his air conditioner could be heard. He scrolled through his phone checking out his social media profiles.

The speed of Mike's scroll slowed as he landed on a throwback Thursday post from Cookie and Chelsea.

The caption read, *My darling baby sister. She was such a firecracker. I miss her…and her smart mouth, dearly.*

A praying hands emoji followed the caption. For a moment, he toyed with the idea of liking the photo.

What the heck? He whispered aloud, as he liked the post and kept scrolling.

He approved a picture that Ben posted from their Vegas trip on his Facebook timeline. Before he placed his phone on the nightstand, he stared at the illuminating Sweet Nothings app on his home screen. Initially, he felt cheap browsing various single women online. However, after receiving a healthy amount of hits on his profile, his confidence elevated.

A SWIPE IN THE WRONG DIRECTION

Even after a few days of browsing, he kept going back to LisaLuck's profile. Truthfully, she had him smitten...and turned on. There was something deeper that drew him in, besides her fabulous physique.

Some would say he was an undercover hopeless romantic. Although he wouldn't particularly classify himself as such, he did feel those first day of school butterflies every time he gazed at her photos. Finally, he mustered up enough nerve to contact her. Worst case, she would ignore him or maybe she had already been swept away by another man.

Hello, you are one of the most beautiful women I've seen in a long time, he typed.

Ugh, where was Tavin when you needed him? Mike was okay on his own, but he needed his friend's gift of gab right now. He erased his message and started from scratch.

Hey, how are you? You are gorgeous and have a beautiful smile. I would love to take you out, he typed again.

Mike put down the phone on his nightstand and then picked it back up and scrolled through Instagram. He was buying time, in hopes LisaLuck would send him a message back soon. After about ten minutes of stalling, he started dozing off.

'Dee-doomp-boom'.

His phone alerted. Mike quickly sat up in the bed. By now, he recognized the alert well. He glanced at the phone and saw a message from Sexxy Jenn. He begged to differ after viewing her profile.

Want a good time? Call me. I'll be waiting 😊

He sneezed and his finger nearly swiped right on the phone. Thank goodness he caught it in time. He quickly swiped left instead. Then, another notification arrived. It was LisaLuck.

A thumbs up to his message. What the heck did that mean? Was that a yes or a no?

He laid his phone on the cold, barren pillow next to him. He wasn't quite ready to place it on the charger yet. Another notification.

Hmmm, well you don't seem like a weirdo and you're pretty cute. I'm free this Friday at 8:00 pm. You pick the place and I'm there, she replied.

Friday couldn't come quickly enough. He spent most of Thursday at work searching for the perfect date venue. He reviewed Lisa's profile again to get an idea. She loved seafood, disliked smoking, was an avid video gamer, and enjoyed action movies.

He found an old school arcade that was right next door to a seafood spot in a trendy area of town. Perfect.

"Mike? Mike? Sorry, I don't mean to disturb you, but I want to give you an update on the streaming report we spoke about yesterday," Marc said.

"Ah, yes. The report. Very thorough. Great work, Marc," Mike replied, as he barely peered up from his phone to address Marc's presence.

"Thank you. I know the email has more granular data than you asked for, but I decided to include our quarter end metrics as well. Do you have any questions?" Marc inquired.

Marc was a smart kid, sharp dresser, and one of the hardest workers in the company. Mike saw tremendous growth in him since he started as an intern two years ago.

"Marc, I'm sorry. I was in my own world there for a second. Yes, I appreciate you supplying the additional data and submitting the report ahead of the deadline. Let's get out of here for lunch today. My treat," Mike said with a smile.

He was a stern boss, but he believed in rewarding his people for great work.

"Sure, sounds good to me. Thanks Mike," Marc smiled appreciatively.

"Don't mention it. Meet me back here at 11:45 am and we'll make a run for it," Mike responded.

He felt his phone vibrating while he was conversing to Marc. A message from Tavin.

Hey man. How do you like that dating app? Any luck yet?

Mike closed the door to his office before he texted back.

Yes, a date this Friday with LisaLuck. #winning, Mike responded.

Ok, I see you. Hmph, I'd say a 'thank you' is in order, Tavin said.

Don't push it. I'll thank you if the date goes well lol, Mike replied.

CHAPTER 6

7:06 pm. Friday night finally arrived. Thankfully, LisaLuck thought it was exciting that they were going to two different locations. Mike's judgment wasn't too bad after all. He sprayed a couple of spritzes of a new bottle of cologne he picked up on the way home from work. It was high past time he created some new memories. He gazed at the old bottle of cologne from Kelly one last time, before he tossed it in the trash can.

7:55 pm. Mike pulled into the arcade a few minutes early. He scanned the parking lot for any semblance of LisaLuck. She was nowhere in sight but then again, he hadn't the slightest idea what kind of car she drove. He decided to go inside to greet her when she arrived. Plus, he wanted to avoid appearing like a desperate creep sitting in his car.

The night air was brisk and cool, but comfortable. The temperature was warm enough to stand outside without catching a chill. Shortly after Mike entered the double doors, he noticed a woman moving toward the entrance. He caught a good glimpse at her face and recognized her;

LisaLuck. She recognized him as well and flashed a flirty grin to greet him as he opened the door for her.

"Well, well if it isn't LisaLuck. You look amazing. So glad to finally meet you in person," Mike said.

She was even more stunning than her photos portrayed. Her hair was shorter, but still shoulder length with some highlights. Her face glowed, with little makeup. Her lips formed an effortlessly delicious pout. He fought the urge to tongue her down right there in front of everyone.

"Please, call me Lisa. I can't let everyone in the street know about my sweet nothings," she laughed. "You're quite handsome yourself. I see that you work out. I like a man that knows how to be physical," she replied, with a welcoming smize.

A magnetic mystery gleamed in her eyes. Mike couldn't put his finger on it, but it made him want her even more. He was totally intrigued by her presence. Not to mention she smelled wonderful, like an intoxicating mix of vanilla extract, warm apple pie, and fresh roses.

"Thank you…..Lisa. I try," he grinned. "So, I know you like video games, but do you have any favorites?"

"Do I? Don't let these freshly manicured nails fool you. I am a Pac Man and Mortal Kombat queen… and don't laugh, Super Mario Cart is one of my favorites too," Lisa replied.

"Nice, no judgment for Super Mario Cart. That's one of my favorites too," he said. "Well, what do you say we get this party started? Ladies first, so you can choose the first game."

"Hmmm….ok, let's see what we have here. Let's take a lap around. This place is huge. Have you ever been here before?" Lisa asked.

"No, it's actually my first time. It's rare to find a woman who has appreciation for video games. I thought this would be a great place for us to try."

Mike led the way as they perused the venue to find the perfect starter game.

"Duck Hunt. We've got to start off here. I haven't played this in ages. Come on, let's go," Lisa said, as she marched fervently toward the console that held the vintage orange gun.

Mike purposely lagged a hair behind so he could get a good glimpse at her backside. Her body was tight, round in all the right places, and voluptuous. She was practically poured into her jeans and the neckline of her fitted blouse rested comfortably on top of her perky breasts. He caught his composure and reminded himself to not appear desperate.

"Don't be a sore loser when I beat you," he laughed.

"Confidence. I like a man that's sure of himself. I'll take it easy on you," she chuckled.

They played five intense rounds of Duck Hunt, with Mike as the victor, before moving on to the rest of Lisa's favorites, including a few newer games. They worked up a good appetite and were soon ready to eat dinner.

Their conversation was effortless. There was no dead silence and they jumped from topic to topic, including marriage (Lisa had never been married, only engaged), politics, religion, career aspirations, and some of their most embarrassing moments.

"I must say, this is one of the most exciting dates I've been on in a long time. I get so tired of the standard dinner and a movie drag. This is different. It's refreshing. Ooh, wait. These hush puppies are not good. The shrimp and fries are delicious; so, I'd give it an 8 out of 10," Lisa laughed.

"Okay. Yeah, I'm with you on that. Not the best hush

puppies I've ever had either. The rest of my food is good," he said and placed the hush puppies in his napkin.

"Alright, so I don't mean to pry but…. don't you hate it when people start off sentences with 'I don't mean to…'? That is exactly what they are trying to do, right? Well, full disclosure, I am curious. How did you end up on a dating app? Got any creepy secrets? Are you a serial killer? Should I make a run for it right now?" Lisa ranted.

Her tone was a bit disturbing. There was a dark sarcasm to her questions, which made for the first genuinely awkward moment of the evening.

"Well, Officer Lisa, if you must know, it wasn't even my idea," he said, with a mischievous smirk, masking the fact that he was taken aback by her abrupt change in demeanor.

"No, you've got to come with something better than that. I'm not falling for the ole 'my phone got hacked' trick," she giggled. Her eyes returned to a softer intensity; less piercing than before.

"I'm serious. Long story short, my friends and I went to Vegas for my birthday last week. I got wasted, my friend took my phone and thought it would be funny to set up a dating profile for me. I didn't know until the next day. I was so pissed at him when it first happened. However, I guess everything happens for a reason because it led me to you," he said.

"Now, that is freaking hilarious. Belated happy birthday. That totally sounds like something I would do to one of my friends. I love a good prank," she laughed heartily.

"So, that's my story. All my cool went down the drain. How did you end up searching for love online? I'm sure there are men lined up at your door waiting for a chance to take you out," he probed.

"You know, the funny thing is most men don't approach me. It's been a while since I've been in a serious relationship. So, I decided I would try something new. I haven't had much success with it yet, but hopefully, that's all about to change now," she smiled.

Mike smiled back as they stared at each other in a comfortable silence for a few seconds. He knew there was something special about her and he was excited for the journey of what was to come.

CHAPTER 7

"Hmmm...someone is glowing this Monday morning. I take it that date on Friday went well. It's a little late for you too. You're usually here well before 8:00 am," Mariah smirked.

"I was running late this morning; nothing to do with my date. However, it was amazing," Lisa replied.

"Well, do tell. Go ahead... spill it," Mariah eagerly waited in anticipation to hear all the juicy details.

"He is actually cuter than his profile, which is a major plus. He's kind and chivalrous, but not a push over. Muscular build. He's witty too. Quick on his feet and he beat me in Duck Hunt. No man has ever done that," she smiled gleefully.

"Duck Hunt? Well, I'll say. Did you get to test out that joystick too?" Mariah chuckled in a low sinister tone.

"See, this is why I can't take you anywhere. Let me get to work. There was no testing of the joystick," Lisa said, shaking her head and scanning the area to see who was nearby. "I'm saving that for next time."

"Ooh, now that's what I'm talking about," Mariah

replied and gave Lisa a high five. Before Lisa settled in at her desk, she could hear her message alert on her phone going off inside of her purse. She settled in, took a few sips of coffee, and scanned her emails before checking her phone. It was Mike.

Good morning, beautiful. I hope your day is going well so far. -The Duck Hunt Champion

Ugh. She was not one to take defeat easily, but she couldn't help but laugh at the message.

I am fabulous, and I hope that you are too. Trust me, you won't be holding that crown for long, sir. I'll see to it that it's a short-lived victory, she replied.

Well, are you up for a rematch on Wednesday night? Mike said.

I don't know about that....I'll have to check my tournament schedule and see if I'm open then. Jk, lol. Sure, I'm down for it. 7:00 pm? she responded.

Perfecto. 7:00 pm it is. I'll pick you up, if that's ok, Mike said.

Hmmm, maybe next time. How about we switch up the roles a bit? I'll come pick you up at 7:00 sharp instead. Does that work for you? Lisa replied, with a sly grin as she glanced up from her phone for a brief second.

Yes, I will be waiting and ready for you, Mike replied.

He thought it was a bit odd that she quickly shot down him picking her up from her house. Nonetheless, her subtle forcefulness was a turn on.

Mike went on about his day with Lisa on his mind. He was excited to see her again before the weekend. Work was a breeze and he felt light on his feet, like he could handle any obstacle in his way. Before he knew it, he reached the end of his work day.

He decided to give Ben a call as he exited the parking garage. His friend texted him earlier, but he didn't have time to message him back.

"Hey, what's going on man? Did your Monday beat you to the ground like it did me?" Ben answered.

"I hate to hear that man. Today was decent for me. Not too bad," Mike said, trying to mask his exceptionally good mood.

"Wait a minute. I know what that voice means. Did Lisa live up to her name? Tell me you got lucky on Friday," Ben asked.

"No, man. We haven't had sex yet, but we are going out again on Wednesday," he said.

"Yet. Confidence. I like it. Keep it up. Hmmm, if she's going out with you in the middle of the week, she's really into you. I'd say you're onto something there," he laughed.

"You and Tavin. I don't know which one of you is worse. I know it's been a long time, but it's not my first rodeo man. I know how to handle a woman," Mike rebutted.

"I'm not saying that. I know you're grown, and you know what you're doing," Ben laughed.

"We'll see how it goes, but I'm enjoying myself and taking it one day at a time," Mike replied.

CHAPTER 8

Lisa opened a bottle of wine and kicked her feet up, as she turned on the TV. The workday was more challenging than she anticipated, so she decided to unwind by watching the reunion episode of *The Real Housewives of Atlanta*. Although she wasn't a huge fan of those types of shows, they boosted her self-esteem. She felt good knowing that she didn't have to deal with some of the issues as the women on the show, despite the scripted antics.

She felt herself dozing off after her third glass of wine. Her phone rang and she scooted over in her oversized chair to answer. The caller registered as an unknown spam risk, so she decided to let it ring. A couple of minutes passed before the phone rang again. The same caller. She purposely ignored it this time.

Lisa eased out of the chair to place the rest of the wine in the refrigerator and surfed through the channels some more until she landed on one of those sappy Lifetime movies. She decided to stop there for a while and kept the movie on as background noise. She wasn't the type of woman to jump at the chance to see a hopeless romance flick. She much preferred an exciting action, drama, or horror movie.

The phone rang a third time minutes later. It appeared to be the same unidentified caller. She answered the phone this time, with a stern tone.

"Yes. Hello?" she said.

"Mmm…hello. How are you? It's been longer than I would like. How have you been?" the male caller stated.

His speech was slow and groggy, like he woke up out of a deep slumber.

"I don't want to speak to you. Stop calling me and move on with your life," she said, quickly agitated by his tone and audacity to call her after all that had transpired.

"That's no way to talk to me after all this time. Don't you think?" he chuckled and taunted her.

"I'm going to call the police on you if you don't stop all of these sick antics. It's over. We're done," she yelled.

She turned too quickly and knocked the empty wine glass off the counter. Pieces of glass shattered on the floor, some of them landing on top of her bare feet.

"Sounds like you've worked yourself up into a frenzy over there. I'll let you go now. See you soon?" he said, in a threatening tone.

"Don't you ever call me again," she demanded.

Lisa was so furious she threw her cell phone at the wall. She swept up all the visible glass on the floor, without cutting herself in the process. After she cleaned up all the glass, her adrenaline was still too high to sit down.

She grabbed a loose razor blade that she kept in the kitchen drawer and held it in the palm of her hand. She was scantily clad, wearing a short, blue mid-drift cropped t-shirt and some short, pastel pink cotton shorts. Lisa punched the top of her thighs furiously, with the razor blade in her left hand.

Then, she grazed the edge of the blade against the top of her thigh, right beneath the hem of her shorts. The razor dug in deep enough to draw blood and she exhaled deeply as she dragged the blade about three inches across her leg. She let out a deep sigh and felt all the negative energy escape her body.

Her phone rang once more, and she felt the muscles in her back tighten. She rose from her chair and grabbed her phone from the floor. She blotted her leg with a few wet wipes to dry the traces of blood. This time, it was Mike calling her. Lisa answered on the fourth ring. She tried to disguise the chaos that ensued moments ago as she greeted him.

"Mike. Hello. How are you?" she said, clearing her throat.

"Oh, I'm doing well. I wanted to hear your voice. Did I catch you at a bad time?" he asked.

He picked up on the awkward tone in her voice.

"No. Not at all. You're fine. I'm glad to hear from you. Today was long, but that's in the past now," she replied.

Lisa continued to patch up the bleeding cut on her thigh with some extra wet wipes.

"I'm here to listen. What happened? Anybody I need to go beat up?" he laughed.

"Hmm, I might take you up on that. It's nothing I'm unable to handle. I hate when deadlines get moved around last minute. That's all. How about you? How was your day?" she asked.

"I'm doing well. Stayed at work a little longer than anticipated today, but no complaints. I found a new place I'd like to take you to tomorrow night, but they don't have an arcade. Is it ok if take a rain check for now on the rematch?" Mike asked.

"Oh, that sounds awesome. I guess great minds think alike because I was going to reach out to you about tomorrow night too," Lisa replied.

"Is tomorrow still good for you? If we need to, we can reschedule," he suggested, hoping that wasn't the case.

"That's not it. I'm excited about our date tomorrow. There's one caveat. I hope you don't mind coming to my place instead of me picking you up this time. Are you up for some home cooking? I can throw down a bit in the kitchen," she replied.

"Sure, I would love that. Let me know what time to arrive. I'll bring some wine," he stated.

"Perfect. The menu will be a surprise, but I think you'll like it. If you can be here by 8:00 pm, that will be great. I'll text you my address," Lisa said.

"Ok, I can't wait to taste your cooking. Well, I'll let you unwind from the day, but I will see you tomorrow at 8:00, Lisa," Mike responded.

He was elated that she was inviting him over for their second date. Things seemed to be headed in the right direction.

"Sounds good. I can hardly wait and hope you have a great night, sir. Thanks for checking on me," she said.

"Likewise, and you're welcome. Hope you sleep well and don't let them work you too hard tomorrow. Goodnight, Lisa," Mike said.

"I will not allow that to happen. They got enough out of me today. You have a good night too," she replied.

Lisa placed the phone on the armrest of the chair and searched inside her refrigerator to get an idea of what to cook for tomorrow night.

Although she was excited about the idea of having Mike over for dinner, the decision was spur of the moment. Honestly, she didn't want to be alone tomorrow night considering the threatening phone call she received that night. At least she would feel a safer knowing Mike would be there to protect her.

She decided to prepare chicken and seafood alfredo for dinner tomorrow. She already had a fresh container of whipping cream, parmesan cheese, and fettuccini noodles at home. All she needed was the meat and ingredients for a strawberry fields salad. She considered ingredients for a dessert as well.

Lisa ran a hot bath and lit several lavender votive candles around the perimeter of her spacious garden tub. Before she turned off the water, she poured herself one more glass of wine. Lisa placed the glass between two of the candles on the edge of the tub. She bathed for over half an hour, as she slowly sipped her glass of wine.

The water helped soothe her mind and wash away her concerns from the day. Lisa felt herself dozing off and took that as her cue to get out of the tub. She dried off, lathered on some peach-scented moisturizer, put on an old Rihanna concert t-shirt, and entered her bedroom closet.

She reached inside a black shoe box stacked underneath a small pile of sweaters on the overhead rack and pulled out her pistol. Lisa placed it under her pillow and fell asleep within ten minutes.

CHAPTER 9

"Ok mam, your total today will be $36.52," the cashier said.

"Ah ok, great. That was less than I was expecting. Nice to get a bargain, right?" Lisa said, as she inserted her debit card in the payment machine.

"Oh, wait. You can get the next person in line. I knew I forgot something. I need to grab some scallions."

"Sure, I'll have everything else in the bag for you right here on the side," the cashier responded joyfully.

Lisa moved briskly towards the produce isle to pick up the scallions. She did a quick mental scan of whatever else she may need to complete the meal for tonight. She was fairly sure the scallions were her only missing item.

As she reached her hand out to grab the scallions, a man quickly placed his hand on top of hers. Lisa stared at him squarely in his eyes, without flinching.

"If you'll excuse me, I'm in a bit of rush. Let go of my hand right now or I will scream. Don't test me. You know I'll do it," she warned.

"Oooh, I'm shaking in my boots. You don't have any

control over me. I love making you squirm. Trust me, if I wanted to harm you, I could have already done so by now. You have yourself a nice evening. Take care," he replied, as he abruptly removed his hand from hers and moved towards the wine aisle.

"Ugh, fuck off," Lisa said, as she stormed toward the cashier.

The lady had finished ringing up someone else and was still standing there as pleasant as can be. Lisa adjusted her expression to not appear rude.

"You're back. For a moment there, I thought you maybe got held up with your male interest. I mean, I'm not trying to be presumptuous. He's handsome. Quite a catch," she replied.

Lisa read the cashier's name badge, before replying.

"Well, Denise, if you must know, he's more of an associate. Not a love interest. In fact, I have a date tonight that I'm cooking for. I'm excited for it. Good men are hard to find, right?" she replied politely, but also in a manner that let Denise know she was getting too personal.

"Oh yes, I totally understand. I am recently divorced, so I am totally done with love; at least for now. That sounds like such a romantic evening. I hope you enjoy the date and your meal turns out delicious," she responded with a nervous smile.

"Thanks, Denise. I'll try my best. You have a great evening. You have been most pleasant," Lisa grinned back at her.

She glanced down at her watch as she moved to her car. Great timing: it was only 5:10 pm, so she was ahead of schedule.

Meanwhile, Mike browsed the liquor store. He wasn't

sure if Lisa's meal would pair better with white or red wine. He decided to get one bottle of Chardonnay and one Cabernet Sauvignon. He was more of a red wine connoisseur, although he enjoyed several different types of white wine.

Mike arrived at home shortly before 6:00 pm. He immediately started getting ready for his date with Lisa. He shaved, showered and tried on a couple of different outfits before he finally settled on one. Mike wore a crisp white shirt, with a maroon vest, jeans and some gray leather Cole Haan boots. For some reason, he was more nervous about this date than the first one. He didn't have to worry about the first impression jitters.

However, he still wanted to look nice for her. By the time he finished getting dressed, it was already a few minutes after 7:00 pm. Mike decided he should head towards Lisa's house in a few, since she lived about 30 minutes away.

Mike took both bottles of wine out of the refrigerator, after they were chilled to perfection. He placed the bottles inside of an insulated bag and left to head to Lisa's house. He texted her to let her know he was on his way. Mike turned on his GPS to navigate to her. He was directionally savvy but didn't want to take any chances on getting lost.

He stopped to get some gas at the corner store near his house. Mike pulled into the gas station to fill up quickly. No one else was there pumping gas, except for a black Infinity coupe that evidently pulled up after he did. Oddly enough, the person never stepped outside of their car. He shrugged it off as the person may have been preoccupied doing something else before pumping their gas.

As soon as he pulled off, he noticed the black car followed him out of the gas station. The person kept a healthy distance. Maybe he or she happened to be going in the same direction. He still didn't think much of it at first until he realized the car was still behind him even after traveling on the highway for 15 minutes. His GPS estimated him to arrive at Lisa's house by 7:55 pm. Perfect timing.

The only thing that troubled him was the fact that this person was continuing to follow him even after he exited the highway. The car followed him all the way until he got about five minutes from Lisa's house. He wondered if it was Kelly. Was she crazy enough to follow him? She did still live near him, so maybe so. He quickly dismissed that thought; she was the last person he wanted to think about tonight. He pulled into Lisa's driveway at exactly 7:55 pm.

Mike decided to wait a couple minutes before he got out of the car. Lisa's garage was nestled behind the generous semi-circle shaped driveway. The front yard was spacious, complete with beautifully manicured shrubs that lined the curb. He parked in the middle of the semi-circle.

Mike didn't see the black Infiniti coupe pass by or lingering near, so he assumed he was in the clear. He deeply inhaled the delicious fragrance wafting inside before he rang Lisa's doorbell. The scent suggested she was preparing something savory and creamy.

Before she unlocked her front door, he heard a loud ruckus in the bushes behind him. If someone was standing straight up, he easily would have seen them. However, the height was perfect enough for anyone crouching down to remain out of plain eyesight. Although the sounds didn't seem to be coming from a small bird or squirrel, he kept his cool as he directed his attention to Lisa, as she opened the front door.

CHAPTER 10

"Hello there, handsome. Come on in. Excuse my apron. I'm almost finished," Lisa smiled.

"You are beautiful, apron and all. It's great to see you and it smells amazing in here," Mike replied. He stood there dumbfounded for a second as he ingested her beauty.

She was dressed in a black, form fitting sweater dress with no sleeves and gold accessories. Mike was a sucker for a sexy shoe: her gold, laced pumps set her outfit off.

"Compliments will get you everywhere, sir. I can take the bag from you. Ooh, nice. A red and white selection. Awesome. It so happens that the meal I prepared goes well with either one. So, I'll let you do the honors," she replied, as she placed both bottles of wine on the counter.

"Ok, I'm usually more of a red wine guy, but I've heard good things about this Chardonnay," he said.

"A man of great taste. I've tried the Chardonnay before and it's delicious. No peeking in the kitchen. I want you to be surprised if you haven't figured it out already. When I first opened the door, I thought you had seen a ghost or something," Lisa stated in a concerned tone.

"Oh no, I'm fine. I thought I heard something in the bushes right before you came to the door," Mike replied nonchalantly.

"I tell you, there's always some rustling out there in those bushes. I know you'll protect me if anything goes awry," she said playfully.

She honestly did feel safe in his presence. She hadn't felt that way with a man in quite a long time.

"Of course, I will. Are you a *Forensic Files* junkie too?" He laughed as he recognized the episode that was playing in her living room.

Her house was tastefully decorated, in a minimalistic, modern style. Shades of earth tones filled the generous space, with a few large pieces of furniture and art. Mike noticed the avant-garde coffee table with bronze tree branch shaped structures for legs, atop a thick auburn rug.

"Ah, you've found my guilty pleasure. I like having it on for a little background noise. I find it so fascinating how those people even have the guts to pull off such crimes.

Anyhow, you came in right as I was cutting the scallions for our meal. Make yourself at home. Have a seat and I'll let you know when to come to the dinner table. This is one of my best recipes, if I do say so myself," she smiled.

"It smells great… my taste buds are eager to experience it," he grinned, with a mischievous smirk.

There was something about the way he worded his statement that sent a tingle down Lisa's spine and a few other places.

"Mmmm, I appreciate that wonderful vote of confidence," she said.

"You're welcome," he said, as she sashayed back in the kitchen.

His eyes followed her all the way around the corner until the living room wall that separated her kitchen impeded any further glances. He inhaled the ambiance of her house. It felt warm, inviting, sexy, yet mysterious (much like her).

He did find it a bit odd that she didn't have any personal photos on the wall or on her tables. There weren't any family pictures around that he could see. He chalked it up to her private mystique and decided it wasn't that important, in the grand scheme of things.

Kelly didn't have any personal photos in her apartment either when they first met. Dammit. He had to block her out of his mind. This was not the time to think about her, even remotely.

"Alright sir, dinner is served. I hardly ever have any company. I can't tell you the last time I've eaten in my formal dining room," Lisa said as she placed each of their plates on the table.

"Your home is beautiful. I hardly have any house guests either, so I feel that much more honored to be here," he replied.

He was impressed by the generous spread and immaculate presentation of their meal. There were two plates of seafood and chicken alfredo, with a zucchini and squash medley, a strawberry and spinach field salad and French bread. Plus, there was a small Corning ware dish of what appeared to be apple dumplings with candied pecans on top.

"My goodness," he sighed in a pleasurable tone.

"I like that smile. I will have you know that everything here is made from scratch, except for the bread and the fettuccine noodles. I hope you don't mind, I poured some of both bottles of wine. I couldn't make a decision," Lisa gleamed.

"Of course not. That's a perfect idea," he said, pulling

out her chair to sit at the table.

"Good. Let's dig in, shall we?" she said.

There was a brief succession of silence as they both started eating their salads. She watched as Mike take a bite of everything on his plate. He then made a second go around of the same pattern. She smiled to herself because he didn't eat all of one thing and then move to the next. It was refreshing to have male company in her house. She could tell he enjoyed her cooking too.

"Everything is delicious. Seriously, this is so good. This sauce is amazing. I can tell it's homemade," he praised her, as he took his first drink with the meal.

He tried the glass of red wine first, since that was his first preference of the two.

"Awesome, I'm glad to hear that. I think I hit the jackpot. The red wine is nice too…it's smooth and a bit woodsy, which I like," Lisa said.

"So, I don't think I ever asked, but are you from North Carolina originally?" Mike asked.

"No, I was born in New York. My dad wasn't fit to be a father back then, so my mom left him. They were married for a couple of years, but they could never make it work, you know. He passed away when I was 6. Shortly before that, my mom decided that New York City wasn't necessarily her top pick to raise a young girl. So, we moved here. I moved away for a few years to Tallahassee for work, but then came back here. Charlotte has been home for me ever since," she said, in between bites of the vegetable medley she prepared.

"Sorry to hear about your father. I'm sure your mother is extremely proud of the woman you've become," he smiled, as he sipped his first taste of the Chardonnay.

"Thank you. I hope she's smiling down on me.

Sometimes I wonder how proud she is. I lost her about a year ago," Lisa replied, as she slightly bowed her head.

"Oh wow, I'm sorry to hear that. I have no doubt she is proud of you," Mike replied.

"Thank you. That's pretty much my life story in a nutshell. I like long walks on the beach. I'm a Taurus…. Your turn. Tell me all about Mr. Mike. I love that name by the way. Every Mike I've known has been a real stand-up guy," Lisa laughed.

"Well, it was between that and Larry. I must say I think my mom made the better choice. I'm originally from Raleigh Durham, North Carolina. I grew up there and lived there until I went to school at USC. That was a culture shock for me. I loved California and even lived there for a few years after I graduated. I learned a lot of valuable lessons there and I do have to give it credit for jumpstarting my career. I could not see myself living in California forever. So, I did some traveling and then moved back here. Charlotte is perfect for me. There's enough of a city feel without losing all of the southern charm," he replied.

They continued to converse about their future career aspirations, college days, pet peeves and some things they want to check off their respective bucket lists. Their interaction almost seemed too good to be true. They didn't have any awkward silences and if there was a pause, it felt natural.

"Alright, so now for the dessert. Hopefully, I was able to pull off a perfectly delicious meal. The recipe is from my grandmother. She used to make the best apple dumplings ever. I added my own flare to it, but I haven't quite perfected the recipe to make them as good as hers. Be honest. Let me know what you think," she said nervously.

"I'm sure I will love it," he replied in an assuring tone,

dipping his spoon in for a generous helping.

"Alright then, sounds like I'm almost there," Lisa laughed.

"You knocked this out of the park. No lie, this is going to be one of my new favorite desserts. Everyone can't make a dumping like this. It's thick and flaky; not too doughy. I absolutely love it. These candied pecans are a nice touch too. Goodness, you are something Lisa," Mike replied, staring deeply in her eyes.

"Aww, thank you. I was more nervous about the dessert than anything. Now I can breathe since you like it. Let me clear off these plates. Would you like some more wine?" she asked.

"Oh no, I insist. Please, relax yourself. The least I could do is clear the table and wash the dishes for you. I must say you have made me raise the bar for whenever I cook for you. I'm going to make sure it's something special," he promised.

"Such a gentleman. You don't have to do that, but I will let you have your way and show my gratitude. Something tells me you are by no means a slacker in the kitchen," Lisa said.

Lisa didn't think he was slacker in the bedroom either. Her mind started wandering as she caught a whiff of his intoxicating cologne as he moved past her. The scent made her temperature rise. Mike's demeanor was more laid back than she was used to. However, there was a quiet strength about him that made her feel safe and secure. That strength also turned her on, as she felt moisture form at the meeting of her thighs.

Mike leaned over her shoulder to pick up her dessert bowl from the table, along with her wine glass.

"Oh, you can leave that. I may have one more glass of

the red wine," Lisa said.

"Ok, I'll save mine too and have another one with you," Mike replied.

He started washing their plates, along with the few dishes in the sink. Everything else that she used to cook with was virtually all clean now.

He abruptly stopped the water and crept up behind her again, this time moving her hair away from the top of her shoulder. His lips connected with her neck softly, inhaling her decadent perfume.

She moaned softly as he sucked on her neck hard enough to leave a slightly red mark.

Then, he stood wide-legged in front of her and greeted her with a kiss on the lips as she rose from her chair.

Lisa kissed him back passionately, gasping for air.

Mike picked her up and sat her down on top of the marble countertop island in her kitchen. He traced his tongue from her neck, down to the top of her left breast. He could feel her heart beating rapidly against his lips, as he groped her breasts with both of his hands – unable to fully cup them inside his palms.

He unzipped the back of her dress as his mouth continued to alternate between both of her nipples. Then, he pulled her dress all the way down to the floor, revealing her matching black lace boy shorts and bra. Mike kissed the inside of her thighs softly at first and then nibbled on her right thigh with his teeth.

She squirmed as he continued to suck on the inside of her thighs. The scent of her made his kisses deeper and more passionate. Mike initially thought she was enjoying it until she let out a sound that was closer to pain than pleasure.

"Is everything ok?" he muttered in between kisses.

He felt a deep scratch on top of one of her thighs. She winced again in pain.

"Um, yeah. It feels good. I just have a little scrape there. Don't stop," she responded, running her fingers in his hair.

"Ok, I won't," he promised, with his lips barely grazing the edge of her left knee.

He slid her lace boy shorts down and grabbed her by her hips to pull her toward him. She gyrated in a circular motion, as he lapped his tongue in her juicy treasure.

"Woooo. Oh, my goodness. You sir…. are…. yeah," she mumbled and tossed her head back in ecstasy.

She swung her right leg over his head so she could sit up from the counter.

Mike had such a firm grip on her hips, she could barely move. He enjoyed the way she tasted and felt against his lips.

Lisa stood up from the counter and pulled Mike's face to hers. She began sucking his bottom lip as she took off his vest and removed his belt.

"Let's move this to the bedroom. Oh, and bring the wine bottle too," she smiled. They had already finished the Cabernet Sauvignon, which was still sitting on the dining room table.

There were candles already lit on the dresser and the nightstands in her bedroom. The aroma smelled like equal parts vanilla, cinnamon, caramel, and rosewood.

Mike grabbed the wine and licked his lips as he savored the taste of Lisa.

"Lay down on the bed," Lisa commanded as she nudged him down at the same time.

She took off his shoes and socks, then slid his pants all the way down. She stood there for a moment admiring his chiseled physique before pulling down his underwear.

Although the lighting was dim, she could clearly see he was standing tall at attention. Her mouth watered in anticipation of what was to come.

Lisa climbed on top of him, with the bottle of wine in her hand. She took a big swig and leaned down to kiss Mike. They traded tastes of the wine between their kisses. She removed his shirt and started grinding her hips back and forth on him. Lisa couldn't resist the urge to feel Mike's pulsating love stick in her mouth before he entered between her legs.

She kneeled before him, as his generous extremity jumped against her lips. She engulfed him slowly and watched for his reactions. The more passionately he moaned, the more she aimed to please. He raised his head off the pillow and then fell back down.

Mike rubbed the back of her neck gently. Lisa massaged his sculpted calves as she crawled back on top of him. A Magnum condom laid on the floor right next to his pants. Lisa was turned on even more.

"I see you came prepared….and well endowed," she said, as she picked up the condom from the floor.

"I um, you know. Wanted to be ready in case," Mike replied, not quite sure how to gauge her comment.

He didn't want her to think he was dating her only for sex. Nonetheless, he wanted her more than ever now.

"Trust me, I don't think that's a bad thing. It shows you're a grown man who knows how to be responsible," she replied. Lisa slid the condom into the palm of his hand.

He quickly put it on, and she was eager to get back on top of him and insert him inside her. He felt even better than she imagined. Mike immediately started breathing hard and gripping her voluptuous behind. He could not believe how amazing she felt.

Mike allowed her to take control a little while longer, before flipping her over on her back. He placed her legs on top of his shoulders as he moved rhythmically inside of her.

She moaned loudly as they continued to pleasure each other for the next half hour or so. They even climaxed at the same time. Kelly was the last woman he climaxed with simultaneously.

CHAPTER 11

The blue light illuminating from Lisa's Alexa speaker woke Mike up out of his sleep. He didn't intend to spend the night and had no idea what time it was now. He gazed toward the window and it still appeared to be dark outside. He would have to skip the gym this morning to make it to work on time, but it was well worth it.

"Mmmm, well good morning to me, Mister," Lisa mumbled, turning over and wrapping her arm around Mike's waist.

"Watch out now. You feel so good, I'll end up missing work to squeeze in another round," he said.

"I gotta hand it to you. You exceeded even my most vivid imaginary thoughts about us together. I understand you have to get going. I want to savor the moment a bit," she said.

"I truly enjoyed you too. The food tasted almost as good as you did," he joked.

"Oh, hush," she laughed. "I aim to please."

Mike moved his hand across the nightstand in the

dimly light room. Two of the candles were still burning, which allowed him to see the silhouette of his cell phone. There was only 8% battery left. He was glad he left the charger in the car.

He felt a sharp edge on top of Lisa's nightstand underneath his phone. He picked up the object and found it was a single razor blade. The placement of the razor seemed odd, but he shrugged off the awkwardness of the moment. Nothing could break his high right now.

"There's plenty of food left if you want to have some for lunch. I've never been good at cooking small portions, even after being single for all this time," she said.

She sat up in the bed and ran her fingers through her hair.

"Hmm, well if you insist, I will take you up on that. Everyone in my office is going to be jealous," he grinned. "I can at least fix a plate for you too for your lunch. Tell me where your Tupperware is."

"It's in the cabinet on the left, right above the stove. That's ok. You don't have to worry about me. I'm going to work from home today. You're such a sweetheart. Thank you," she replied.

"Nice, I should have planned to do the same. I am not fit for going into the office today…. thanks to you," he said, as he strode naked from the bedroom towards her kitchen.

Mike left his phone on the nightstand. He was so put off by the razor blade there that he never actually picked up his phone. He heard his 5% battery life alert sound off. Lisa yawned as she laid on her stomach, glancing in the direction of the phone on his side of the bed.

Another alert sounded and Lisa instantly knew what it was. The dating app. She felt a little disgusted when she heard the alert. Although she and Mike weren't exactly exclusive, the alert reminded her that he may be seeing other women.

What if he was playing with her emotions all along? What if he wanted sex and never called her again? Whatever. She couldn't dwell on it. Worst case, she did have a few amazing orgasms in the process. Her body needed that. She stared at the phone once more and exhaled deeply.

"Is everything ok?" Mike said, as he entered the bedroom again.

"Oh yeah, I'm okay, other than recovering from you. I have some big reports to get in today so I'm dreading that. But it will be good. No worries," she replied.

"I'm sure you will knock it out with flying colors. Thanks again for…well, everything. I'm going to get on the road now so I can get home in time to get ready for work. I thoroughly enjoyed you. I'll call you later," he said, smiling and rubbing his hand across her cheek.

His touch made her knees shiver, as she rose out of the bed to see him out. He grabbed his cell phone from the nightstand before he left her bedroom.

"That sounds like a plan. I enjoyed you too. It's been a while since I've felt this comfortable and excited about a man. This is new, but it feels so good. I'm loving it and taking it day by day," Lisa exclaimed.

"I am too. This is such a refreshing feeling for me as well," Mike replied.

He finished getting dressed and put on his shoes before he wrapped his arms around Lisa one last time. He squeezed her waist and kissed her on the forehead before he grabbed his food and left.

Lisa shut the door and sighed deeply. She felt exhausted

and energized at the same time. Love had proven to not be her friend in the past, but maybe she finally would get it right this time. Only time would tell. In the meantime, she climbed back in bed and hugged the pillow that Mike slept on. She inhaled the remnants of his scent and pretended he was still there.

CHAPTER 12

"Well, I hate to say it but let's take a shot to 'I told you so'," Tavin said, as he tossed his shot glass back.

Lisa and Mike had been dating for a couple of months now. However, Lisa was out of town for the weekend, which freed Mike up to hang out with his friends on Friday.

"Here you go. I said thanks, man. What more do you want?" Mike laughed, as he gulped his shot.

Ben watched the two of his friends as if he was watching the dramatic climax of a good movie. He loved playing the instigator.

"You know, if it wasn't for Tavin, there would be no you and Lisa. I'm glad you were able to get out of the house. She must have some really good…" Ben exclaimed before Mike cut him off.

"Wait. What do you mean able to get out? The calendar aligned perfectly. I would still be here right now even if she was still in town," Mike replied, anticipating their antagonistic reaction.

"Get out of here. Please," Tavin shrugged.

"Yeah I have to agree with him. You found out she was going out of town a couple of weeks ago, right?" Ben asked.

"A few days ago, but what does that have to with anything?" Mike rebutted.

"Oh, it has everything to do with it. You reached out to us on Wednesday to see if we were free today. I bet you had to make sure that her travel plans were still solid," Tavin replied, in a sarcastic tone.

"Alright, alright. I'm into her. She's amazing and the truth is I would have never met her without your, ahh… 'help'," Mike sighed.

"There's the spirit. Seriously, it's getting heavy between you two. Do you think you might be moving a little bit too quickly?" Tavin inquired.

"No, we're not rushing anything. It's not like I'm about to propose to her tomorrow," Mike responded.

"I think what Tavin is trying to say is live your life man. I know it's been a while since you've been in a serious relationship. I mean, you've kinda been chasing Cookie for years but she has way too much drama. Between her and Kelly, you haven't had your share of reckless fun in a long time. Or maybe not reckless, but hell, harmless fun. Are you ready to get tied down into something so deep again?" Ben asked.

Although Ben was the youngest, his words resonated with a certain wisdom that caught Mike off guard.

"I get it. I know you both are concerned. I promise, I'm not going to get into something crazy. Cookie was different. She is different. She's special, but I know it's not going to work. Lisa is a good woman and I'm happy with her," Mike said.

"Cookie is special alright. Let's drink to good women.

A SWIPE IN THE WRONG DIRECTION

We're happy for you man. The one question I want to know is how are you handling the dating app now that you are semi-serious with Lisa?" Tavin asked.

"Yeah, about that. I didn't see the need for it anymore, so I inactivated my profile," Mike admitted.

"Whoa, this is serious. Did you decide to delete it on your own or did she influence you to do it?" Ben asked.

"I'd say it was a mix of the two if I had to be honest," Mike said.

"Lies. Let me tell you how it went down. She told you that she felt uncomfortable about you still having the app on your phone. She heard the alert going off on your phone, got a little insecure, and decided to "influence" you to make the decision on your own to get rid of it. Oh, and I bet it was right after you had sex," Tavin relayed.

"She did admit to me that it made her feel uncomfortable, so I thought it would be best to get rid of it. She never asked me to. I did it on my own," Mike replied.

"No, no, no. Mike, did you even check to see if she deleted her profile? I'd be willing to bet you it's still active," Ben said, shaking his head in disbelief.

"There's only one way to find out. Let's see for ourselves," Tavin said, as he pulled up the app on his phone.

Mike knew his friends meant well but he often felt like they were two annoying brothers that gave him unsolicited dating advice.

"Was his namo. See for yourself," Tavin said, as he turned the screen of his cell phone toward Mike.

A cloud of uncomfortable silence hovered over the table. Mike saw it as clear as day. LisaLuck.

CHAPTER 13

Mike woke up the next morning without the alarm clock. He liked to sleep in a little on Saturdays since he was usually up by 5:30 am during the week. His sleep was somewhat interrupted, due to his conversation at the bar with Ben and Tavin.

He didn't want to admit it to his friends but seeing Lisa's active profile made him feel uneasy. He wasn't necessarily angry, but, her still active profile did make him feel uncomfortable. Ironically, he thought about deleting the app on his own right before Lisa mentioned it. She happened to beat him to the punch.

Nevertheless, he tried to shrug the thoughts off and got out of bed to start his day. He turned on his Bluetooth Bose speaker and selected one of his Spotify workout playlists. Mike brushed his teeth as the music played. The weather was forecasted to be perfect that day, so he thought it was a great opportunity to go for a run outside.

He put on some Nike shorts and a tank top, grabbed his ear pods, cell phone, a bottle of water, and exited the front door. He stretched on the sidewalk before the start of his run. As he selected a playlist, he realized he missed a call from Lisa. He typically called her right back if he missed her call. Today, he decided to let her wait until he finished his run.

The weather outside was beautiful. The air was brisk and cool. Mike took a moment to admire the yellow, auburn and green colors of the leaves changing to usher in the upcoming fall season. He exhaled deeply before he picked up the pace on his run. Running kept his mind clear. It was convenient for him to run by his house because there was a trail less than a mile away. The full trip around the trail was shy of four miles.

Mike bumped into his neighbor, Mrs. Middleton, about two miles into his run. Their interactions were a bit awkward, mainly because she was so nosey – and because he slept with her before he started dating Kelly. Mrs. Middleton was older than Mike, by about 10 years, but she never wasted time telling people about her estranged husband. Mike never met the guy, but he still felt bad that he technically slept with a married woman. Nonetheless, the sex was amazing.

"Well, hello there, handsome. Isn't it a gorgeous day for a run? I see great minds think alike," she smiled happily, with her chest pushed forward.

Mrs. Middleton, or Rachel, as she preferred to be called, was attractive and aware of her good looks. She wore her hair in a short-cropped bob, with blonde streaks. Rachel's eyes were hazel and almond shaped. Her olive-toned complexion was flawless, and her supple lips formed an effortless pout. Her pink and black sports bra was low cut and cupped her full breasts perfectly. Her midriff was slightly exposed, and her shapely legs filled her black and yellow tights.

"Rachel. Good morning. How are you on this great Saturday? It's good to see you," he replied, with exaggerated gasps for her.

He hoped that would deter her from any lengthy conversation.

"Why, yes it's good to see you too. I hope you and your new little girlfriend are faring along well. She's quite the catch. Young love – as easy as the first day of spring," she winked at him.

"Thank you. We're not rushing into anything and taking it one step at a time," he answered in a matter of fact tone.

"Oh, yes. I am by no means suggesting that your love for each other is superficial. I didn't mean to interrupt your run. You had a good stride. Don't be a stranger. You're more than welcome to come by any time for a visit," she grinned seductively.

"I'll have to do that sometime," Mike blatantly lied. "Well, it was good bumping into you here, Rachel. Hope you have a great rest of your weekend."

"You too, Mike. Take care now," Rachel replied, as she sauntered down the trail.

Mike glanced down at his watch to check the time. 10:49 am. He rounded out the remainder of his run and made his way back home in less than 15 minutes. Despite his setback with Rachel, he still made fairly good time. As he entered his home, he finished the rest of his bottle of water and grabbed a couple of slices of pineapple from the refrigerator.

He connected his phone to his Bluetooth speaker and dialed Lisa, as he sat on his kitchen stool. He had to muster up excitement to speak to her.

Why was her Sweet Nothings profile still active, especially after she questioned him about his? he thought. Mike waited anxiously.

"Well, good morning handsome. I was afraid that maybe you were busy and I had missed you. How's your morning going so far?" Lisa inquired.

Was she questioning his whereabouts? Did she think he was dodging her call? How could she even remotely suggest such a thing when she still had her dating profile up, live and well. Mike's mind raced with numerous questions.

"Not at all, babe. I got back in from a morning run and saw I missed your call. How did everything go at the gala last night?" he asked.

"Oh, it was wonderful. I sent you a picture of the award I received. I got the 'Excellence in Perseverance' award; it was totally unexpected. At least I know all my hard work lately hasn't been in vain," she said.

"Most definitely. I can't think of a woman more deserving. That is awesome. Congratulations. Sounds like a celebration is in order when you get back. Have you had a chance to connect with Gina yet?" Mike inquired.

"Thank you, baby. I'm down for a celebration with you. Yeah, I'm about to check out of the hotel here in a bit and meet her for lunch. She's such a hoot. She talked a mile a minute when I spoke to her last night. You'll have to meet her one day. I think you will love her," Lisa replied.

"I've heard nothing but good and slightly reckless things about her, so I'm sure I will," Mike laughed.

"Well, I don't want to hold you finishing up your workout. I feel like I need to be doing the same after the heavy meal last night. I'll let you know when I get out of here and make it Gina," she replied.

"Ok, babe. Sounds good. Be careful," Mike said.

Although they were both into each other, neither one of them had said 'I love you' yet. Mike wasn't sure what her reasoning was, but he assumed it was too quick to convey that type of feeling for each other. As far as Mike was concerned, he could see himself falling in love with Lisa.

However, there was still a piece of him that wanted to hold on to his independence. He didn't want to fall too hard and lose himself in another relationship. He was too old to go through that again.

✦

Meanwhile, Lisa packed up her things for checkout. Gina texted her to let her know she was in route to pick her up from the hotel. She was relieved that she wouldn't have to catch an uber to her house. Plus, she was hungry. Her breakfast consisted of a few sliced pineapples and yogurt with granola. Although Gina told Lisa she would be there in about 10 minutes, Lisa was all too familiar with Houston traffic. 10 minutes meant 20.

Lisa tied up a few loose ends for work on her laptop before she headed down to the lobby. Gina called her as she was exited the elevator. She was parked in front of the double entry doors leading to the lobby. Lisa and Gina hadn't hung out together in about two years. They were nearly inseparable in college and kept in touch, despite the many blows life threw each of them.

"Girl, you are always so put together even in the morning. Ugh. I'm sick of you. Come give me some love," Gina bellowed as she threw her arms around Lisa to embrace her with a tight hug.

"Stop it. You are gorgeous. It's so good to see you, girl. It's sad that it took a work conference to get us together again, but I'm glad for it," Lisa smiled, as she loaded her bags in Gina's trunk.

As soon as Lisa got in the car, they immediately started catching up and cracking jokes, like old times. "So, first things first. Where are we going to eat lunch?" Gina asked, excitedly.

"I see some things never change. I can't blame you. I'm hungry too. You can pick the place," Lisa replied.

"Alright then. How about Maggiano's? The nearest one is about 15 minutes from here," Gina said.

"Oh ok, that will be about 30 minutes then. Girl, I don't see how you live here. I know Charlotte operates at a much slower pace, but geez. This city is moving and going nowhere fast at the same time," Lisa laughed.

"Hey, I had to go where the money was. You know, they're almost turning me into a Texan. The way I drive, we'll be there in 20 minutes tops. I know a back road we can take," Gina rebutted.

"You, a Texas girl? I'll believe that one when I see it. So, what's been up? What's new? Who's new?" Lisa chuckled.

Her friend was a nonsense woman in relationships and dating. However, her quick dismissal of men cost her some good men in the past.

"You know what? I've decided I'm going to be a lesbian. Want to give it a try?" Gina said nonchalantly.

"Um…I don't think I know what to say. For the first time, I am at a loss for words with you," Lisa laughed nervously.

"Lighten up. When was the last time you got laid? I was playing. I have had no luck with the last two guys so I'm taking time to work on myself; whatever that means," Gina added.

"Amen to that. There's nothing wrong with putting yourself first. Women shouldn't be made to feel that they need a man to complete them. It's time out for that," Lisa agreed in a matter of fact tone.

"Umm, hmm. Alright Ms. Female Liberation. You still didn't answer my question. When was the last time you got laid? Judging by that blinding glow, I'd say it was sometime recently," Gina said.

"Alright, if you must know I am dating someone. It's getting a little serious. He is…. whew. He's something else. I'm enjoying the moment, without any expectations," Lisa said.

"Do tell. I need details. Spill it," Gina said. Her exaggerated hand gestures coupled with her wide-eyed stare further cemented her anticipation.

"Um, mam, let's not die today on the highway. Focus, please. I'll show you a picture of him when we get to the restaurant."

"I'm so happy for you; seriously. If anyone deserves it, you do. I know for a while you were nervous about getting back out on the dating scene. I can't say that I blame you. You're such a strong woman. Still standing as beautiful and vibrant as ever after all the tragedy," Gina smiled.

CHAPTER 14

"Let me give you a piece of advice, sweetie. No woman is going to wait forever for you to decide you're fully over Kelly. A woman in her 30's especially won't stand for it. I never did, even with your father or any man before him. How old is Lisa again?" Mike's mother inquired.

Mike decided it would be a good idea to mention his budding relationship with Lisa to his mother. He was still a bit perturbed about her currently active dating profile, but nothing was perfect. If it was the only flaw he could find about her, he still felt like a winner. His mom continued to ask him whether he had a girlfriend or not. Mike thought if he casually mentioned Lisa, that would get her off his back. He was sadly mistaken.

"Hey Mom, I appreciate the insight. She's 32. I'm not trying to overthink this. I'm taking my time and seeing how things go. Maybe you'll get to meet her one day, if I keep her around long enough," he replied.

He was still trying to be respectful, but he was ready to get off the phone. Mike glanced up in his rearview mirror and noticed a car tailgating him that was similar to the black Infiniti that followed him on his way to Lisa's house. He still heard his mother's voice, but his mind was preoccupied. Maybe it was all in his head, but something seemed strange.

"Hmmm, I'll be waiting then. We will see. I'm glad that you have someone to keep you company in the meantime. I know I've probably said more than my peace by now. I'll let you get back to your day. I made a new friend at the church and I'm going to meet her for a late brunch. Her daughter is gorgeous. She's single, but they have a bit of an estranged relationship. I don't know what's up with that. She's been quite tight-lipped about it. I suppose she will tell me in her own time," Mike's mother replied.

Mike paused for a moment. The car was still behind him. Whoever it was must have been traveling in the same direction he was. It didn't necessarily mean he was being followed.

"Mike, are you there? Did you hear me?" his mother asked.

"I'm sorry mom. Yes, I did. That is great about your new friend. I'll have to meet her soon. I know you're concerned about me. I don't take any offense to it," he responded.

"Well, that's good to know. You enjoy yourself and Miss Lisa," she said.

"Alright, I will. Enjoy the brunch mom. Love you," Mike said.

"Love you too," his mother replied.

Mike hung up the phone and turned his music back on. He tilted his head toward the rearview mirror again. The car was gone. He let out a quick sigh of relief as he pulled into the parking lot of Best Buy. A Bose sound bar that he had been eyeing for a few months finally went on sale and he decided to purchase one for his living room. He stayed on top of the latest and greatest techno gadgets.

He quickly found the soundbar once he stepped inside. The checkout line was longer than he expected, even for a Saturday. Mike was glad to wait in it though. It was shaping up to be a good weekend, even though it was his first without Lisa. He didn't want to lose his identity being with her. Their time apart was refreshing. Nonetheless, he did miss her presence.

Mike inhaled the beautiful day outside, as he moved to his car with his new sound bar. The strong rays from the sun created strange glare on his car's back window. He stepped closer and saw that his glass was shattered. He ran to assess any other damage that may have been done. The rest of his car appeared to be ok.

He unlocked the car to find a fire engine red brick laying in his back seat. It's always something. He knew today felt too good to be true. He scanned the parking lot and spotted a young teenage girl sitting in her car. She was parked a couple of rows behind him, so she would have had a good eyeshot of who vandalized his car.

"Hey, excuse me young lady," Mike said, tapping on her passenger side window.

Her music was up loud, and she was so enthralled in her phone that she didn't even realize he was standing there.

"Get the hell away from my car," she yelled back at him.

"Wait. Can you turn down the music? I need to ask you a question," he said, pointing towards his car.

She followed his gaze to the broken back window, as she reached forward to turn down her music. She rolled down the window wide enough to hear him clearly.

"I'm guessing that's your car over there. I'm no snitch, but I'm sorry that happened," the girl said in a sassy tone.

"Ok, well this has been productive. You have a good day," he replied, as he marched briskly back to his car.

The young lady beeped her horn loudly to get his attention as she rolled down her window to give him the details of what she saw.

"Well, I guess I can't be a snitch without seeing a closeup of his face. All I know is he was tall, kinda thin and he was dressed in all black. He even had a black hoodie on. He had a bit of a beige skin tone but with a bad tan from what I can see. At least if you see some guy on the street in all back, you can narrow it down to whose ass you need to kick," she said.

"Yeah, that does narrow it down a bit. Thanks. I appreciate you telling me what you saw," he replied.

"Sure, sir. Hope you're able to track him down," the girl responded.

"I'll get it fixed and everything will be back to normal in no time. Have a great day," Mike told the young girl, as he turned back toward his car.

The teenaged girl rolled the window up and turned her radio up high as she drove off the parking lot.

Mike sat in his car for a moment before he pushed the ignition button. He put his head on the steering wheel in frustration and scanned the parking lot for any other semblance of foul play to give him a clue about the person who damaged his car. He reached in the backseat and knocked the glass off the top of the brick. He picked it up and flipped it over. A message at the base of the brick read, "Your end is near."

CHAPTER 15

"Evie, it's so refreshing to meet someone like you at the church. I'm so glad we ended up serving on the welcome committee together. I mean, a lot of the other women at the church are so..." Jeanine's voice trailed.

"Oh, let me finish that sentence for you. Stiff? Some of those women act like being a Christian means you can't let your hair down, have fun or even a mimosa or two," Evie laughed, raising her glass to toast with Jeanine.

Evie loved to entertain, but today she decided to invite Jeanine over for a special girl's day with the two of them.

Jeanine admired her new friend. She loved how she was so carefree, with no inhibitions. She was so confident and comfortable in her own skin. After Mason died, Evie lost some of her social ease and grace that she once had as a married woman.

"Stiff as a board. Yes, that's it. You can say that again. Evie, can I ask you a serious question?" Jeanine inquired.

"Sure, ask away. I'm an open book," Evie replied.

"Well, how long did it take you to get over your husband

when he passed? I can't seem to find my groove since he's been gone. I used to be so much more confident and carefree. Now, I feel like I second guess everything," Jeanine sighed.

"You know, that's a loaded question. I may seem like I'm all polished and bulletproof, but I'm not. I'm a fragile woman at my core, but life has a way of giving you a hard exoskeleton. When Ted passed, it took the life out of me. Soon, I had a new problem that made that one minute. My own daughter. She still doesn't speak to me. I don't know what got into that girl, but I'm as good as dead in her eyes. I never hear from her. That's been my worst pain of all. I feel like if I can survive that, I can survive anything," Evie replied solemnly.

Jeanine wanted to sink under the rug on the floor. She knew Evie and her daughter had a strained relationship, but she didn't know it was that bad. Her feelings of unworthiness and social awkwardness felt so insignificant now. At least she could say that Mike loved and appreciated her. He never acted ashamed or ungrateful. She was more blessed than she ever realized.

"Evie, I'm so sorry. I didn't realize things were that strained between you and your daughter. I'm sure she will come around soon. You're an amazing woman and a great mother. It's only a matter of time before she comes to her senses," Jeanine said.

"I'm going to remain faithful that day will one day come. I decided that I'm going to live life to the fullest. However long I have left, I want every day to be intentional. Do you know what I mean?" Evie asked, as tears formed at the corners of her eyes.

Jeanine never saw her friend in such a vulnerable light.

"That's the best way to live. I'm trying to adopt that mindset now. I wish I had lived my life that way in my younger years. Would have saved myself a lot of unnecessary heartache," Evie said.

"No heartache for the rest of our days. I'd say that's cause for another mimosa. Now, what's going on with that son of yours and his new mystery girlfriend? Have you had a chance to meet her yet?" Evie asked.

"I haven't seen her, only heard about her. They've been dating for a few months now. After his last relationship, he's been extra cautious. I guess he wants to have all his ducks in a row this time. I can't convince him that love is about risk. He has to learn on his own. He's been much happier lately, so I'm grateful," Evie said.

She felt extremely uncomfortable now, filling Jeanine in about her son's exciting new love interest. She decided it might be best to deflect the rest of the discussion from herself.

"Isn't that splendid? Young love is so ravishing. Perhaps his new love interest could give my daughter some tips on how to treat people, namely her mother," Evie replied sarcastically.

"Hmph, well who knows if she'll even stick around long enough for that. I'll keep you posted," Jeanine shrugged.

✦

"Baby, come on. Is there anything else wrong?" Lisa asked, rubbing her foot on Mike's leg as they cuddled on the couch watching TV. They both were big fans of *American Horror Story* and decided to catch up on the latest season.

"Oh yeah. I'm fine. I hate that prick got away with smashing my window. I've been trying to let it go. It could have been worse. I don't want it to ruin our night," Mike said.

Lisa had been back in town for a couple of days. She spent her time back in town at Mike's house.

"At least you didn't get hurt. Plus, you have insurance too, so that's good. I feel like you're a bit distant tonight. That's all," Lisa replied.

"Oh, really? Well, I can't keep pretending. It's not me at all. There's something I need to discuss with you," Mike said in a serious tone, reaching up to grab the remote to pause the show.

"Um…..ok. Go for it. What's on your mind?" Lisa asked, with her arms folded in a defensive stance.

"You know how you kinda asked me to remove my dating profile a while back?" Mike replied.

"Shit. I already know where this is going. Mike, I'm so sorry. I owe you an apology. I assume you saw that my profile was still active. I deleted it on my way back. I swear I didn't even realize it was still active until I haphazardly mentioned it to Gina," she said.

"I'm confused. How did Gina prompt you to delete it?" he asked, relieved that she deleted the profile, but still agitated.

"I didn't think that would be your response, but I was telling her that I like you and things are getting serious. She knows I've tried dating apps and that's what prompted me to go and delete it. I can see how it may seem like I had a double standard with you inactivating your profile. I promise it wasn't anything like that," she said.

"Oh wow, well thank you for letting me know. So, things are pretty serious with us, huh?" he joked, trying to lighten the mood.

He could see the guilt and shame written all over her face and didn't want to make her feel any worse.

"Um yeah I'm not spending all this time with you for the fun of it. Hey, there's something I need to tell you too," Lisa replied.

"Uh oh, I don't know if I should brace myself," he laughed.

"Hopefully, you won't find this too alarming. Mike, I think I'm in love with you," Lisa confessed.

"What would you say if I told you that makes two of us?" Mike asked, leaning in to give Lisa a deep, passionate kiss.

All his anger toward her evaporated between their lips. He hadn't felt so enamored about a woman in a long time.

CHAPTER 16

"I don't know about all this, man," Ben said, as he shook his head. He glanced down at his poker chips before making his move. The guys had monthly poker game nights, which were off schedule a bit in the last couple months. Tonight's game was at Mike's house. A few of the other guys had already left. Only Ben, Tavin, and Mike remained.

"Wasn't this the goal of you and Tavin's brilliant plan back in Vegas?" Mike said.

"Yes, to an extent. We wanted you to get out and have some fun. Explore your options. Slap a little ass, multiple asses even. Don't get me wrong. Lisa seems like a great woman. A little high strung, but nice. Are you ready to marry her though?" Ben asked.

"Dude, we're not 25 anymore. I don't have any kids and I'm in my mid-thirties now. It's time to make that next step. We've been together for over six months. How long do you think we should stay in a relationship?" Mike asked.

"Hmph. Do you actually want me to answer that? I love my freedom man. I don't plan on getting tied down any time soon. You're more of a relationship guy. So, I get it," Ben rationalized.

"I'm thinking about introducing her to my mom next month for Thanksgiving. It's about that time. They've spoken on the phone a couple of times now and they seem to be hitting it off well," Mike said.

"Yeah they're hitting it off well now because you aren't married yet. Wedding cake sours all marriages. It's a proven fact. Shit goes downhill as soon as you say, "I do". Make sure you're doing this for the right reasons, Mike. Not because you feel like it's the right time or you're getting pressure to do it," Ben said.

"Man, for someone that's never been married and seems to lack the desire to ever get married, you sure know a lot about it," Mike laughed.

"Hey, you don't have to bite a donut to know it's sweet, do you?" Ben chuckled.

"Whatever, man," Mike replied. He couldn't help but laugh too.

"Well let me get out of here. Unlike you, my app is still alive and well. I'm meeting up with Lucinda tonight and I'm quite sure it's going to be a good night," Ben said.

"Lucinda? Are you sure you're not meeting up with somebody's aunt?" Mike laughed.

"Laugh now brother but wait until I send you her picture. If she is somebody's aunt, then I'll be glad to lay in auntie's bosom for the night," Ben responded.

"Oh, damn. I see the pic now. Alright then, Lucinda. You let me know how that turns out. I'll live the rest of my single days vicariously through you," Mike said.

"Gladly. I'm up for the challenge. Holler at you later man," Ben replied.

"Man, I know it's a weeknight so I'm going to get out of your hair too," Tavin added, as he followed Ben to the door.

"Alright, fellas. You both have a good night. Hope you both get lucky and share the details, when you do," Mike laughed.

Mike turned on some music while some ESPN highlights were muted on the TV. The couch called his name. He grabbed a left-over slice of pizza from the food he ordered for the group before taking a seat. He was so glad tomorrow was Friday. However, Mike couldn't help but question whether his friend was right about moving too quickly with Lisa.

He felt like he loved her. She had her ways; but overall, she made his life better. Plus, the sex was spectacular. He didn't have any unfulfilled needs in that area. Mike genuinely could see himself settling down with Lisa. Nonetheless, in the back of his mind, he was somewhat cautious of completely falling for her.

Mike's phone vibrated as it rang on the kitchen counter. He didn't race to go pick it up and continued to eat his pizza. Lisa already told him she was working late tonight, so he was nearly certain she wasn't calling so soon.

The phone rang again. Mike decided to see who it was this time. The call was labeled as a spam risk. He picked it up on the fourth ring anyway.

"Yes. Hello?"

Dead silence.

"Hello? Can you hear me?" Mike repeated. Again, no audible sounds from the other end.

"Don't call this number again," he said, in a frustrated tone.

"Be careful," a distorted, deep male voice replied.

"Excuse me. Who are you and how did you get this

number?" Mike asked, as he leaned on the granite countertop of the island in his kitchen.

"Consider yourself warned. Your precious little Lisa isn't who you think she is. Watch your back," the man said.

He hung up the phone before Mike was even able to respond.

CHAPTER 17

"I am so nervous. My palms are sweaty, and I barely slept last night," Lisa said timidly.

"Baby don't worry about it. I promise. She is going to love you. Trust me; it's going to be ok. There's not much family left on my mom's side now so she will be ecstatic to have the company. Your potato salad is amazing too. Hell, if she doesn't like it, that's more for me," Mike joked.

"You always know the perfect thing to say. Babe, are these pants too tight? I think I'm going to change and then I'll be ready to go," Lisa said.

She obsessively tossed her hair between her fingers while she stared in the mirror.

"Lisa, your pants are not too tight. Thick thighs save lives. Umph," he said, smacking her on the butt as he moved past her.

"Sir, I'm trying to make a good first impression; not turn you on. I guess it will be okay. My shirt is long enough," Lisa convinced herself.

Mike loaded his cornbread dressing and Lisa's potato

salad in the backseat. He double checked to make sure everything was off in the house and then went to the bedroom to get Lisa. He saw her smiling excitedly as he entered the room.

"Well, somebody's mood is lifted. What's got you beaming over there?" he asked in a playful tone.

He felt a little uneasy, though he tried not to let it show. Ironically, his phone buzzed next and he checked the message on his smart watch. Cookie sent him a 'Happy Thanksgiving' message. He decided to respond to her later.

Mike had a quick flashback of the mysterious person who called him to say Lisa wasn't who she thought he was.

Could this be what the unknown man warned him about?

He tried to brush the thought out of his head, but to no avail. Nonetheless, he had to refrain from letting Lisa read his uneasiness.

"Oh, it's Gina acting up, like her usual self. I told her I was a little nervous and she made me laugh. She sent me some crazy gif of some crazy woman in the street, running frantically in circles with rollers in her hair. That girl hasn't changed a bit. It was good catching up with her last week," Lisa said.

"No good laugh is in vain. I'd like to meet Gina soon. I know she's one of your best friends. After all, you've met Ben and Tavin already. You're pretty special if you still want to stick around after meeting those guys," Mike laughed.

"Your friends are harmless. They are some funny guys. Gina, on the other hand…. that girl is a hoot. I'll see when she can come up here to visit and let her know to be on her best behavior," Lisa said.

Lisa and Mike got in the car and started on their short journey to Jeanine's house. She lived about 30 minutes away. As they eased down the highway, Lisa's anxiety waned as she conversed with Mike.

"Do you know how I can ease my tension and relax?" Lisa said.

"I have a few things in mind." Mike replied, with a mischievous grin.

"Mmmhmmm. I bet you do. I want to hear some of those cute, little embarrassing stories about you as a little boy. I'm sure your mom has some adorable pictures of you. Ah, I can't wait to see them. I know you had to be the cutest kid ever," she continued.

"Hopefully, those pictures are locked away in safe keeping, never to see the light of day. Those are not 'Lisa-proof'," he chuckled.

"Don't worry. I'll still think you have swag. We all have to start from somewhere," she laughed.

They continued to joke with each other and listen to music on the way. Before they knew it, they arrived at his mother's house. Her rose garden in the front of the house was starting to bloom quite beautifully.

Lisa felt a shudder down her spine as Mike parked the car in the driveway and turned off the ignition.

"She is going to love you. I'm telling you. Trust me," Mike assured her. She loved that he was able to read her mind so easily.

"Wooo. Alright, if you say so." Lisa replied.

She pulled down the visor to inspect her makeup one more time. The last thing she wanted was to have lipstick smeared on her teeth or a piece of hair out of place.

Jeanine opened the door before Mike even had a chance to ring the doorbell.

"Oh my, let us give thanks," she said as she hugged Mike tightly.

She embraced Lisa as strongly as Mike and ushered them both inside.

"Mom, it's great to see you. Mmmm, it smells delicious in here," he said.

"That's music to my ears. Hopefully, it tastes as good as it smells. Mike, your description of Lisa did not do her justice. You are gorgeous, darling," Jeannine said, as she shifted an approving gaze toward Lisa.

"Oh, you are far too kind. Thank you. It's a pleasure to meet you in person Ms. Jeanine. I see where Mike gets his striking good looks from," Lisa replied in a chipper tone.

Mike could tell she already felt welcomed. He was quite sure his mom would love her.

"Mmmm. Well, flattery and good potato salad will get you everywhere in life," Jeanine said, as she lifted the lid of the container to peek at Lisa's dish.

"It's a special recipe. I haven't made it in a long time, but I figured this was the perfect festive occasion to bring it out of hiding," Lisa said.

"Well, come on in. Let's not keep our appetites unfulfilled any longer. Lisa, make yourself at home. Mike, I think you still know your way around," Jeanine said, as she patted Mike on the back.

"Oh mom, did you do some remodeling in the kitchen? The tile is nice," Mike asked.

"You're right. I sure did. I wanted something different. I think it brightens up the kitchen a bit and gives the house a warmer feel. I've been trying to do some things for myself and live more; not be so uptight. Oh, here's a picture of my new friend, Evie. We tried to take a 'selfie', like you young kids do," she laughed.

"Oh yeah, I remember you telling me about her. I'd say

you nailed the selfie. What do you think, babe?" Mike asked Lisa, turning the phone towards her.

"Oh, um yeah. What a wonderful picture. Everyone needs a good selfie and that one is spot on. You look so pretty Ms. Jeanine, and so does your friend," Lisa replied.

There was a bit of an awkward pause from Mike and Jeanine, following Lisa's response. Her energy seemed a bit oft put.

"Please darling, call me Jeanine. Evie would have been joining us for Thanksgiving, but she had a bad migraine earlier. She told me she would call me and stop by if she felt better," Jeanine said.

"Well, that's good. Who wants to be lonely on Thanksgiving?" Mike said, with a concerned tone in his voice.

"Lucky for her, lonely and Evie are like oil and water. She's been through a lot, but she keeps a bright spirit. I shouldn't be telling her business, but can you believe her only daughter doesn't even see about her? The girl is here somewhere in North Carolina, at least that was the last thing she knew. Lisa, can you imagine someone being so selfish and cruel? I can't believe it," Jeanine ranted.

"That is horrible. Who could do such a thing to their own mother? Sounds like her daughter is missing out on a relationship with a great woman. Evie seems lively and fun," Lisa said, as her voice trailed off.

Mike noticed the flushed, pale tone that loomed on Lisa's face. Her demeanor seemed troubled and uneasy. It was the first time Mike had seen that expression on her face since they went inside his mother's house.

"Well, I guess we should all dig in," Mike suggested.

"Yes, that sounds like a great idea. If you don't mind Ms. Jeanine, I would love to fix your plate. You said you don't cook much, but something tells me you were busy preparing this wonderful turkey, cabbage, mac 'n cheese, and the peach cobbler," Lisa exclaimed.

"Thank you, sweetheart. That is so kind of you. Evie tells me I should live in the moment, so I guess I'll take her advice. Sure, I don't mind if you fix my plate. Thank you so much. Mike, I think she's a keeper," Jeanine winked and smirked as she sauntered into the kitchen.

She came back with a tall, yellow pitcher filled with her homemade Arnold Palmer.

Jeanine genuinely liked Lisa for her son. She thought she would make a beautiful wife and sweet daughter in law. However, she tried to compose herself and not embarrass Mike.

"Babe, I'm going to give the potato salad one last quick whisk before I put it on the plate. I can fix your plate too. I assume you want a little bit of everything?" Lisa asked.

"Oh baby, I can do it. Or how about I fix your plate then if you fix mine?" Mike asked, while he leaned in to get a kiss from Lisa.

He was happy that his two favorite women were getting along so well. They all gathered in the dining room together and started enjoying the food.

"Ooh, Lisa, this potato salad is fabulous. Mmm, it has the right amount of mayo too. Some people put too much, but this is perfect," Jeanine said.

"Oh, thank you. Your turkey is so moist. I can never get mine to turn out so juicy. I love spicy food, and this has the right kick," Lisa added.

"Yes, everything is so good. It's nice to get a break and relax and eat. Lisa and I have been so busy on the go lately. Yes, Mom, she is a wonderful cook too," Mike replied.

They all continued to fellowship and watch TV for a few hours before Mike decided it was time for him and Lisa to leave. His heart felt at ease seeing his mother. Maybe hanging out with her new church friend, Evie, gave her a new spark. They helped her clean and get the kitchen back to normal before they left. Jeanine insisted that they pack some to-go plates home and Lisa saved some of the potato salad for her.

"Well, you all have truly made my day. This has been a wonderful Thanksgiving. Mike, thanks for coming to see about an ole lady. Lisa, it was an absolute pleasure meeting you. Before you leave, let's all take a selfie. I bought one of those selfie sticks so we can get a good one," Jeanine said.

"Oh, well my hair is a mess today. I don't know if I should be caught on camera like this," Lisa said, with a nervous expression plastered on her face.

Her complexion turned pale again, like it did earlier.

"I won't hear of it. You look beautiful. Come on, we'll take one then you all can be on your way," Jeanine smiled. Lisa didn't feel like taking a picture.

However, she wanted to continue to make a good first impression with Mike's mom.

"Ok, are we all centered? Say cheese," Jeanine commanded with excitement.

CHAPTER 18

"Oooh, baby I do not want to get out of this bed. You're so lucky you don't have to go in today. Mmmm, I would much rather stay here with you," Lisa moaned, as she rolled away from Mike's chest to get out of bed.

"I know, babe. I thought you didn't have to work a full day, though," Mike said.

"Well, technically you're right. I'm not holding my breath on it," she said.

"I know what you mean. Well, I have a few errands I need to run after I leave the gym, but I'll keep my lunch plans open in case you are free," Mike added.

"That sounds good, babe. I'll keep my fingers crossed. I'm going to jump in the shower, love. Maybe we can go to the movies tonight? That new *Saw* spinoff should be good," Lisa replied.

"Oh yeah, that sounds like a plan to me. Great suggestion, babe," Mike said.

His phone alerted as soon as she stepped into the shower. It was a text from a local number that he didn't have saved in his phone.

You don't know me, but I have connections with the Charlotte Police Department. I need to speak with you today. It's pretty urgent.

Mike stared at the phone for a minute before he typed anything back. "Are you still enjoying the lap of luxury from the bed in there?" Lisa said, from the shower.

Mike was in a bit of a daze from the disturbing text message and took a moment to respond.

"Oh yeah, baby. Not for long. I'm about to get up in a minute," he said.

"Mmmhmmm. Hey, I don't blame you. Don't get up now on my behalf," she said, form the shower.

Mike typed a quick text back to the anonymous sender. *Excuse me? Who is this?* No response.

"Well, there's one thing I can think of that's better than staying in bed while you get ready for work," he said, sitting up in the bed.

"Oh, okay then. Hmmm, I wonder what that is. Can I have a hint?" she asked playfully.

"I'm sure I can show you better than I can tell you anyway," Mike said.

"Alright, I won't argue with that," Lisa replied as she turned off the shower and reached for the towel.

She leaned closer to the edge of the tub before she noticed that the towel was missing from the rack.

"Searching for this?" Mike said, as Lisa stepped out of the shower.

She planted both feet on the ground and faced him. He stood completely naked with a towel draped across his shoulders.

"Damn, nice towel there, mister," Lisa said, as she

surveyed his chiseled body with her eyes.

Her nipples hardened as she moved in to embrace him. A vibrating tingle quickly formed at the meeting of her thighs.

"I'm glad you like it. Why don't you let me dry you off?" Mike grinned, as he bit his bottom lip.

He flipped the towel from around his neck and used it to pull around Lisa's waist to bring her closer to him. They both fell on the bed together, kissed, and groped each other passionately.

Mike loved the dampness of Lisa's body fresh out of the shower, mixed with her natural moistness. He moaned as she inserted him inside of her and rocked back and forth, steadily. She exhaled in ecstasy as he thrust himself deeper inside her. Mike sat up and pushed himself against the headboard of the bed, while Lisa instinctively wrapped her legs around his lower back.

The two continued to move in a sensual rhythm, until Lisa couldn't hold it any longer. She exploded all over him. Mike flipped her on her back, while she was still shuddering. He pulled her legs up on top of his shoulders. Mike stroked slowly at first, then rapidly; unable to contain himself. He exhaled deeply as she breathed in his heartbeat on her chest. Mike kissed Lisa softly on the side of her neck. Then, his phone dinged with two new text message alerts.

CHAPTER 19

She's a schemer. Consider yourself warned.
You should leave while you can......if you are smart.

Mike stood there stunned at the new text messages he received from the creepy anonymous person. Lisa had been gone for about an hour. He had a hard time wrapping his brain around the fact that some stranger was questioning Lisa's true motives with him. There was no way this could be true. He felt it. He knew their relationship was real. No one could convince him otherwise.

He stepped away from the phone to pour himself a tall glass of orange juice. He decided to turn on the TV to take his mind off the texts. He hadn't even responded yet. There was nothing that he could say that would make sense.

The phone rang. He stood up from the couch to see who it was. Surprisingly, it was his mother. She knew he was off work today.

"Hello? Hey Mom. How are you?" Mike answered. He attempted to disguise the angst in his voice from the situation at hand.

"Oh baby, how is my boy doing? Make sure you tell that sweet Lisa I said 'hello' if you're with her. I don't want to interrupt anything if she's around. I remember what it was like to be your age; young and in love," she said.

"I'm doing well mom; at home relaxing a little bit before I get out to run a few errands. I'm the only one here, but I'll let Lisa know you said hello," he replied.

"Oh, good. Mmmm, I taught you so well. I usually wouldn't admit something like this, but this cornbread you made is even better than mine. It's delicious," she exclaimed.

"Thank you, Mom. I learned from the best. Is everything okay?" Mike asked. He could sense there was more to her phone call than she was letting on to.

"I can't get anything past you, can I? There is something I do want to let you know. Now, I don't want to cause any dissention between you and Lisa. I don't know what to believe. I showed Evie the picture of us from last night. She came over for a bit after you left," Jeanine said.

She paused for a moment before she continued.

"Ok, that's good she came over. How is she doing? Is she feeling better now? he said.

"She's a lot better now, physically at least. I wish you could have seen her face when I showed her that photo of us. She started crying, Mike. Hard. I didn't know what to do. According to her, the girl in the picture resembles her daughter closely. Are you sure Lisa's parents are dead?" Jeanine asked.

Mike was speechless.

"Mom, I don't know what I'm supposed to say to this. Do you think maybe Ms. Evie believes Lisa reminds her of her daughter? Lisa's parents are dead. She told me so herself," he said.

Everything he thought he knew seemed unstable now. He couldn't let on to his mom how disturbed he was by her news.

"I thought that you should know. Keep this to yourself for now. Things like this have a way of surfacing on their own. You know? I want you to be happy. You do know that, right Mike?" Jeanine pleaded.

The guilt in her voice for dropping this secret was audibly heavy on her heart.

"I know, Mom. I'll get to the bottom of it. I promise, I'll be fine." he assured her.

However, he had no idea what getting to the bottom of it even meant. This wasn't an easy situation to uncover.

"I love you. You're a good man, like your father. Never be so good that you miss the smoke and mirrors. Trust your gut instinct. It usually won't steer you wrong," she replied.

"Thanks, Mom. I love you too. Hey, I'm going to get out for a bit to get a little fresh air. I'll talk to you later. I enjoyed you yesterday," he said.

"Ok, baby. You know I enjoyed you too. Hey, don't you go and do anything you'll regret later behind this girl. You still have the rest of your life to live. Don't let a bad decision ruin your future," Jeanine cautioned.

CHAPTER 20

Mike waited at the back of the Barnes and Noble. It had been only ten minutes, but he decided to get a hot cup of tea while he waited. He didn't favor the taste of coffee. He checked his watch again – another five minutes passed. He was starting to think that maybe this was a bad idea after all. Maybe it was all a hoax.

A man dressed in a navy-blue long-sleeved shirt, jeans and brown Aldo boots stepped in. His hair was cut short and he had a bit of an after five shadow: not a full beard. Mike had a hunch that was the guy he was supposed to meet. He was right.

"I assume you are Mike?" the man asked.

"Well, you know what they say about assumptions. Exactly who are you?" Mike replied defensively.

Obviously, the man had an advantage over Mike with the information he supposedly knew. He wasn't going to willingly provide any additional information.

"Fair enough. My name is Marc. I'm a retired police officer. I have some information for you about Lisa that you may want to hear," he said.

"This all came out of the blue. What's your angle here? How did you find my information?" Mike asked quietly, as not to draw attention to them.

"Well, we will get to that a little later on," Marc replied.

"No. Let's get to it now. I'm a little busy today, so let's cut straight to the chase," Mike replied in an agitated tone.

"Alright then," Marc replied with a sarcastic smirk. "I used to date Lisa. She's a dangerous woman. You should be careful of her. She's a big reason why I stepped down from the police force. Her and those pricks in my department. That is neither here nor there," he continued.

"Oh, that makes sense. You don't seem to be old enough to have retired from the police academy. Seems a little suspect," Mike said.

"Yep, I'll be 43 in a couple weeks. Listen, Lisa has tried to run schemes on several men before to get money. She even tried it on me, but I was one of the ones that got away, literally. Also, I believe she may have been involved in the death of her first husband. I couldn't find any hard proof," Marc ranted.

Mike's eyebrows furrowed as he listened to the man's accusations. His stomach started turning flips inside.

"Oh, wait. Did she not tell you she was married before? I guess some things never change," Marc smiled.

"How do you know all this? How do I know you're not making this all up? I should have never come here," Mike said, as he abruptly stood from his chair and gulped the last sip of his tea.

The tea was still warm and slightly burned his throat on the way down. That was no comparison to the burn his heart felt from hearing the shocking information about Lisa.

"I can imagine you're upset. You know there's some truth to what I'm saying. I don't take you to be anybody's fool, which is why I think you came here today. I'll let you be on your way. Review this and don't let her see it or know that I gave it to you. Enjoy the rest of your day, Mike," Marc said as rose from the table like he had won a championship boxing match.

"Yeah, you too," Mike replied.

He glanced at the folder before he grabbed it and exited the Barnes and Noble coffee shop. On one hand, he was infuriated that Marc had the audacity to speak about Lisa in such a vile way. On the other hand, he was afraid of the potential validity to Marc's story.

As fate would have it, Lisa called him on his way home. He pretended like nothing was wrong.

"Hey, baby. How is your day going? You think you may have some time to sneak away for lunch?" Mike asked.

He had honestly forgotten about their tentative lunch plans, but he remembered as soon as Lisa called him.

"Hey babe, it's going pretty good. I was calling you about lunch. I can go this afternoon but that means I'll have to be here another three hours. I think it might be best I have lunch delivered here and keep working. Then I can leave in a couple of hours. I'm ready to get out of here and see you. Sounds like you're out and about. Don't do anything fun without me," she laughed.

"Oh no, baby. Never that. I'm out running a few errands and about to be home soon myself. Well, I understand about lunch. I know work has been a beat down lately. How about we stay in tonight and I cook dinner for us?" Mike suggested.

"Mmm, I love you. Yes, that sounds perfect. I can't wait.

Well, I'll get back to it so I can get done with everything here. Oh, you didn't tell me exactly what it was that you were out doing?" Lisa asked, with a tinge of innocent curiosity.

Dammit. Why did you have to ask that? Mike thought.

Obviously, he couldn't tell her his where he was.

"I'm actually on my way to the grocery store now. I cleaned up around the house a bit earlier and dropped a few old things off at Good Will," he responded.

"I see you, Mr. Productive. That sounds good. Hopefully, you get some down time in there to relax and soak up the day a bit too." Lisa suggested.

"I will make sure to do that baby. Can't wait to see you later," Mike replied.

"Me neither. I'll let you go for now. Love you," Lisa said.

"Alright then. See you soon. Love you too," Mike replied.

He let out a long sigh of relief after he ended the call.

CHAPTER 21

Lisa massaged the back of her neck to ease the tension from the work day, as she drove to Mike's house. Something gave her an uneasy feeling at the pit of her stomach since late morning, but she couldn't figure out why. Nonetheless, she turned on some music to shake it off. She would see Mike soon and then all the troubles of the day would be a thing of the past.

Meanwhile, Mike was watching TV at home on the couch. He tried to act like everything was fine. So much had changed since the morning. Mike dropped the files from Marc off at his office at work, after he scanned them. He didn't want to take a chance of leaving it anywhere within arm's reach of Lisa.

Then, he heard the garage door open. It must have been her. She told him about an hour and a half ago that she would be leaving in about fifteen minutes. Now, he questioned the validity of everything she said. He breathed in deeply and exhaled slowly as he heard her shut the car door.

"Honey? I'm home…..finally," Lisa said, as her voice

trailed off a bit.

"Hey babe. Did you have to work longer than you expected?" Mike inquired, as he stood up from the couch to greet her.

"Mmm, something like that. I did have to work a little longer than I expected. Then I had to play counselor to Allyson. That girl is unbelievable. Although, she did give me a nice compliment. She said I have been glowing ever since we started dating. I thought that was nice," Lisa replied.

"You know I've been known to have that glowing effect on women," Mike laughed.

He could barely keep a straight face when he made the arrogant remark.

"Is that right? Ok, well I am the lucky one because I am getting that glow all to myself right now. Aaahh…, I'm so glad to be done with this day," she said, as she placed her bag down on the counter, while Mike moved in to kiss her.

"No, I'm the lucky one to have you. Here, I had this ready for you when you got home," Mike said.

He handed her a cocktail he made.

"Yes, this is what Friday nights are made for. This is delicious, babe. Thank you so much. I know it took me longer to get here, so I totally understand if you would rather go out to eat tonight," she said.

"Nope. I already have the food prepped. Dinner should be ready in 20 minutes. You sit down on that couch; rest your feet and I will handle the rest. How about that?" Mike replied with a smile.

His stomach fluttered as he tried to keep pretending everything was okay.

"Sure, that sounds great, if you don't mind. Let me get out of these clothes and get comfortable," Lisa replied.

"Sounds good babe. I'll get started on the food."

He grabbed the food out of the refrigerator and started preparing it. Mike was thinking of something tasty, but simple. Lisa mentioned Chinese food several times lately, so he decided to whip up a quick stir fry. He mixed the shrimp, diced chicken breast, peas, carrots, candied pecans and water chestnuts in a wok. He finished quicker than he expected.

"Oh, my God. Babe, that smells so good. A little sweet, savory and spicy mix there?" she asked.

"Yeah, I would say something like that. It's practically done. Maybe another 10 minutes. I hope you enjoy it," he said, after he poured a little more of the homemade honey Asian ginger glaze that he made over the food.

Mike served up his prepared dish and another cocktail to Lisa, while she was sat on the couch watching TV. She raved about how good the food was, as they made small talk with each other.

"Mmmm, babe this hit this spot. You know what? I think you're a keeper," Lisa laughed.

"So glad you enjoyed it. I made it with you in mind since I know you've been having a taste for Chinese food lately. I hope you want to keep me around. Otherwise, you've wasted about 9 months of your life," he chuckled.

They laid together on Mike's plush sectional couch, sipping on the rest of their drinks.

"Let's see what's on Netflix. Wanna watch the last season of *Ozark*?" Lisa suggested.

"Oh yeah, that sounds good. I've been waiting on that one. Let's go for it," Mike replied.

He hugged Lisa from behind her waist as she sat in front of him on the couch. They both fell asleep before the first episode was over.

Lisa woke up first and prepared to wake Mike up to tell him to come to bed. He slept harder than normal. She smiled as she rubbed his face while she hoovered over him. She grabbed both of their phones from the table. Lisa accidentally opened an unread text message when she picked up the phone.

She quickly closed out the screen, but only after she read the message.

Did you review the files?

The source was from an out of town number. Although she didn't recognize the phone number, she had a suspicion of who the sender was. There was only one person she knew with that 786 area code.

CHAPTER 22

Mike felt the sunlight peering through his bedroom curtain. A metallic taste filled his mouth and he felt like he had a hangover. He knew that couldn't have been possible because he only had two glasses of wine last night. He groaned as he turned to his side, but realized his hands and feet were tied up to the posts of the bed. The whole room was a floating blur. Lisa was nowhere to be found.

"Mmm, babe. It's a little early to be playing kinky games. Lisa?" Mike called her name.

Complete silence. His head felt cloudier the more he moved.

"Oh, yes darling. Did you send for me?" Lisa answered in an unfamiliar tone.

He could tell she was close by, but he still couldn't see her in the room. His vision was highly impaired. Then, he saw a trace of her silhouette as she glided into the bedroom. Mike wasn't sure if his mind was playing tricks on him or if she was dressed in all white.

Lisa moved closer to the bed and Mike's focus started to

get clearer. She was not only wearing all white, but a full out wedding dress. Something shiny and red glimmered in her left hand. An apple. She took a bite and stood over him, as she reveled in the bewildered expression on his face.

"Um, babe, this isn't funny anymore. What's going on? Why are you dressed like that?" he asked.

"Why am I dressed like this? Isn't this what you wanted? Oh, come on. I know you've been thinking about it. I searched through your laptop and saw some of the ring selections you bookmarked. You have great taste, I must say. Ah, but that's neither here nor there at this point," she paused, as she took another large bite of the apple.

"Why would you……?" Mike muttered.

His energy dwindled even more.

"Oh, wait. Don't speak. Conserve your energy. Let me say it for you. How could I do something like this? I must be crazy and out of my mind, right?" Lisa responded.

Mike gazed back at Lisa in amazement and fear. Lisa wasn't acting anything like the woman he fell in love with. He had no idea was what about to happen next, but he figured his best bet was to cooperate with whatever she said.

"Men. So predictable. Guess you should have been a wee bit more careful with your text messages. You're an honest guy, though. I know you're not trying to hide anything from me. Such a noble trait. Gullible as hell, but noble. I see that you've become acquainted with Marc. Good ole Marc. He's the one that got away…. literally," she laughed.

"Marc was sweet, at first. He was nothing like you. You, good sir, have been the sweetest so far. He had this one female friend that I knew he was way too close with. He swore up and down that he didn't sleep with her. Men lie to me all the time. I can sniff it out. I never caught him, but his slutty little friend was the one that tipped him off to me. She was the one that exposed me and made me appear as if I was only after his insurance policy. Of course, that was part of the plan, but I didn't need that little cunt revealing it so soon," Lisa confessed, in an irritable tone.

"I thought you were different. I can't believe I fell for somebody like you," Mike retorted. He became visibly agitated with Lisa.

"Now that was pretty hurtful. Somebody like me, huh? That wasn't too nice of a thing to say. You know what? You hang tight babe. I'll be right back," Lisa said, as she lifted up the bottom of her dress to prevent it from being swept under her feet.

Mike mustered up the little energy he had to attempt to free himself from the bed posts before she came back in the room. He wiggled hard enough to create some give in the knot on his left wrist. He scooted over to loosen it with his teeth.

He focused in on the paper weight on his nightstand; it was dense and heavy. He needed something loud enough to create a disturbance for help. The window. It would be a hard reach, but he could possibly break the window if he threw it hard enough. He heard Lisa rustling through the garage. He had one shot to throw the paper weight hard enough to break the window.

The paper weight shifted on top of Mike's leg and nearly toppled off the bed. Thankfully, he caught it before it hit the floor. He had to make his move now. He grabbed the contoured groove of the paper weight and squeezed it firmly in his hand. The garage door slammed, as he threw the paper weight at the window with all his might.

CHAPTER 23

Lisa scurried into the room, as she continued to lift the bottom of her dress with her right hand and a steak knife from Mike's kitchen in her left. Mike slipped his hand back inside the knot in time for her not to notice an immediate difference in his position. The window cracked, and a few chips of the glass broke. However, the alarm didn't sound.

"What the hell have you done? I thought I told you to stay put?" she yelled.

A few more pieces of the glass chipped. Finally, the alarm went off. Mike laid there silently, staring at her.

She ran back towards the living room and attempted to silence the alarm. She tried three combinations, including his birth day and month and two variations of his favorite numbers, three and seven.

"How the hell do I turn this shit off? What's the code?" Lisa screamed at Mike.

"It's…the….," Mike's voice trailed off.

He purposely answered her slowly, as he hoped to buy enough time for the police to arrive. Whatever she sedated him with had nearly worn off now and he was almost completely coherent.

"Answer me. What is the code?" she asked again, with much less impatience than the first time.

"Your birthday," he muttered.

"Sweet. We have to turn this off now," she said, running back to the front door to turn off the alarm.

"It's not working."

"Oh, that's because it's your real birthday, 0502, not 1107. Crazy bitch," he laughed hysterically.

Although he remained in a compromising position, he smiled with joy as knew that the police would arrive any second.

Lisa opened and closed the front door to silence the alarm. The sound still blared loudly. She surveyed Mike's living room in a frenzied state. Lisa swiftly raised the knife that was still in her hand and dragged it on the side of her forehead. She stopped right above the downward curve of her eyebrow and tossed the knife in the sink. Her adrenaline was so elevated she barely felt the sting of her broken skin.

"Hands up," the officer commanded as he barged through the cracked front door.

Lisa accidentally left it ajar in her fit of rage when she tried to disable the alarm. Another officer followed closely behind the first, gun pointed forward, as he scanned the room. Blood poured from Lisa's right temple.

She brought her hand up to her bleeding wound as she cried, "Help. Help me, please. I know he didn't mean to do it. I was trying to protect myself."

She fell as if her legs had been clipped from underneath her.

Mike finally freed himself of his ties and slowly rose

from the bed. He moved carefully into the living room.

"I'm innocent. She did this to me. She tied me up," Mike uttered.

He was perplexed about the streak of blood on Lisa's face, and shocked that she went to such great lengths to appear that she had been hurt.

"Get down. Now. Get on the floor. Hands up," the other officer commanded.

Mike stood there dumbfounded, unable to move.

"Are you deaf, boy? We said get down. Right now."

Lisa watched in disbelief as she continued to cry from the floor. Then, the deafening shot was fired.

The officer that initially crossed over the threshold from the cracked front door mistakenly pulled the trigger.

Mike tried to move out of the line of fire, but he was hit in the chest.

Mike slumped to the floor as he gasped for air. A pool of blood formed underneath him.

"No. No. No. Come on, baby. Get up. Get up for me, please. You don't deserve this," Lisa said.

"Mam, we need you to move back. He can't hurt you anymore. You're safe now," the officer spoke.

The officer that didn't pull the trigger stared at his partner in awe. He acted as if he did not even realize that he potentially killed a man based on instinct alone.

"I didn't mean for all of this to happen. He was going to be my husband. We were going to be together forever," she continued to sob.

The ambulance arrived minutes later. Lisa watched as they lifted Mike's lifeless body from the floor. She was lifted on a separate stretcher, but she never took her eyes off him. Her head started to swim, and she suddenly felt nauseous.

CHAPTER 24

"Tim, get in here man," Officer Will Fields said.

"What's up? I'm about to head out for lunch. This better be good," Tim said.

"Ugh, I don't know how good it is. I think we messed up, more than we know, with that guy and his bride to be in the wedding dress. You gotta admit that lady was strange, even for a situation like that," Will replied.

"What exactly are you getting at?" Tim replied, as he took a seat, with a perplexed expression on his face.

"Check out this file. It was left at the victim's office. I know it's only been a few days. Everything is still early, but this can turn things around for this case," Will said.

"Hmm, I'll examine it during lunch. Besides, if we dig into this, we both could go down for it. You know us shooting that guy was a mistake anyway. The woman was clearly abused, no matter how quirky she may have seemed," Tim replied.

"Oh, so now we pulled the trigger?" Will responded.

"Keep your voice down. You know what I mean. I

promise, I'll check it out as soon as I get back. Want me to pick you up anything for lunch?" Tim asked.

"I'm good, but thanks man. I don't have much of an appetite right now," Will said.

He picked up the folder again after Tim marched away. He couldn't rest until he connected the dots in Lisa and Mike's incomplete story.

◆

Lisa's hand shook as she held the test. She put it down and picked it up again. Positive. It was her third one in the last two weeks and they all gave the same result. She was pregnant, with Mike's baby. She let out a deep sigh and grabbed a razor blade from her bathroom counter.

Lisa laid across the bed and rubbed her stomach. She smiled as the tears glided down the sides of her face and into her ears. She graced the blade across her right wrist, hard enough to scratch her skin. A booming knock at her door suddenly jolted her out of her trance. She wasn't expecting any company, so she quickly threw on some sweatpants and a t-shirt.

"Yes, who is it?" she said as she tip-toed toward the peep hole.

"This is Officer Fields. I need to speak with you about Mike Bryce."

"Ok, sure," she responded curtly.

Although her heart sank to the bottom of her feet, she did not allow her anxiety to surface. Lisa opened the door and welcomed the office inside.

"Hello, we investigated Mike's background closely. We wanted to make sure he had not abused any other women in his past. His mother swore up and down he would never hurt a fly. Unfortunately, that's something nearly all mothers say about their sons," he said.

"Abuse? Yes, um there weren't any clear signs of it before that night. I was terrified. It was like he flipped out or something. Still haunts me when I go to sleep at night. I know he didn't mean to do that. I choose to believe that he was out of his head," she said.

"I can only imagine how traumatic that experience was for you. Did he ever mention his involvement or interaction with any ex-girlfriends?" Tim asked.

"I knew he was getting over a broken engagement when we met. Other than that, I wasn't privy to anything else," she replied.

"Okay, I see. Was he ever married before, to your knowledge?" he asked.

"Oh no. Neither one of us have been," she replied as her voice trailed off.

"So, you've never been married?" Tim asked.

Lisa was getting agitated, but she tried to keep her poker face.

"That's correct. Never been a bride," she confirmed.

"Ms. Wilmington, we have good cause to believe otherwise. You're under arrest for the murder of your ex-husband, Nate Aspen. Anything you say can and will be used against you in the court of law," he said, while placing her in hand cuffs.

He forcefully ushered her outside. Evie waited anxiously beside the police car. Perhaps it was a mix of women's intention and a mother's love that confirmed her daughter's guilt. Evie never forgot how agitated Lisa was when she first divorced Nate.

She never received a straight response from her daughter on what drove her marriage to implosion. Shortly afterwards,

Evie saw a report of his death on the news. When she confronted Lisa about the tragic incident, her daughter's response was cold and unbothered. After months of probing, Lisa abruptly stopped speaking to her mother.

Lisa eyeballed her mother with a gaze that pierced straight through her heart, before she lashed out at her.

"You did this? You back stabber. How could you? I hate you," Lisa screamed.

"Lisa, I didn't do a thing. How could I? I'm dead, according to you. Remember?"

Evie returned the same cold stare back to her estranged daughter.

EPILOGUE
One Year Later (Swipe Left)

Mike's legs felt like vertical lead structures, as he made the hardest walk of his life. The generous aisle felt like it was closing in with each step. A calloused lump formed in the back of his throat as he witnessed Bill's head in his hand and slumped shoulders. Mike always knew Bill to have perfect posture. Today was a more-than-worthy cause for his countenance to crumble.

I can't do this.

Mike coached himself as he moved closer to the pearl-colored casket with golden handles. A single tear raced down Mike's cheek as he peered inside to view the love of his life. So many emotions overcame him. Sadness, fear, depression, and anger flooded his mind.

He softly brushed his hand against Cookie's arm as he marveled her natural beauty, even in death.

Her shoulder-length signature bob was cropped to perfection – with all its auburn highlights still intact. Her eyes had just a hint of eye shadow and her cheeks were just slightly blushed to contrast her complexion. Cookie's lips donned a naked gloss, with an expression that insinuated her soul was lifted.

Mike turned to find a seat, as he firmly shook Bill's hand. Sheila and Sean were seated right next to him, with their new baby in their lap. Sheila tried her best to hold in her hysterical tears, while Sean tended to the baby.

However, Breanna shattered Mike's heart. Although she was not crying now, a numbed look of sadness filled her eyes. Her eyes were the splitting image of her mother – almond shaped with exaggerated dips at the corners closest to her nose.

Mike was about to take his seat on the second row when Bill gestured for him to come forward.

"You sit here with us. You're family," he demanded.

Mike was honored that Bill requested his presence with the family. He hoped no one else felt awkward by his presence in the family section. To his surprise, Breanna looked up and gave him a genuine, wide-mouthed smile. That soothed his pain for a moment.

The next 30 minutes seemed like a blur. Mike's front row seat forced him to look at the spray of beauty roses surrounding Cookie's casket. Her sudden death seemed so unreal, like an episode of *The Twilight Zone*. Before he knew it, his time had come to speak about his dearly departed love.

Mike cautiously approached the podium, as he tugged at the hem of his black suit coat. He exhaled deeply before he uttered his first words.

"I think I speak for us all when I say time is not kind. I am not ready to accept that Candice, or Candy as I often called her, is gone. So, I will not use "was" because her energy is still here. Candice is an extraordinary type of woman. Her presence always commands the attention of the room and she has a glow that lights up everyone she encounters, including me. She gives, uplifts, encourages, inspires, and blesses us all with just one of those radiant smiles of hers. Today, I choose to take that smile with me wherever I go, and I pray you all do the same. Thank you," he concluded.

He was showered with claps and several standing ovations, including Bill. Mike felt proud to honor his close friend, despite his resentment for being unable to love her as he truly wished. As he looked toward the back of the church before he took his seat, Mike noticed there was standing room only. He spotted Ben and Tavin a few rows back, who both offered supportive nods for his speech.

"That was really pretty what you said about mom," Breanna grinned, as she wiped the tears from the corners of her eyes.

"Thank you, Breanna. I'm so glad you think so," Mike replied, as he hugged Breanna with his right arm.

He wondered how a child so young could comprehend the loss of her mother. Did she really understand Cookie was gone? Deep down, Mike felt she knew.

"Yes, incredibly beautiful. Mike, do you mind coming with me into the foyer for a moment?" Bill requested.

"Sure, of course," Mike said, as he rose from his seat again. Another wave of anxiety covered him as he stood and avoided looking inside the casket again.

"I'm going to make this brief, but there's something I need to tell you," Bill said, as he and Mike stepped in the middle of the vacant foyer.

Mike paused in anticipation, unsure of what Bill was preparing to tell him.

"Candice told me that you and she have been on some

dates in the past few months. Life is a funny thing. Who knew this aneurysm would come and take her out like this? Both of my girls and my wife are gone now. You need to know that Cookie loved you. She told me there was something different about you and she hated she didn't realize it sooner."

"Thank you, Bill. That's um.... wow. You have no idea how great that is to hear," Mike replied, with a slight crack in his voice.

"You're welcome, son. Truth be told, I have been pulling for you for quite some time. I just thought you should know how she really felt about you," Bill said.

"I deeply appreciate hearing this. I really do," Mike responded, with his eyes filled with tears, as he clenched the engagement ring in his left pocket.

CARLOS HARLEAUX is an author, poet, publisher, blogger, and speaker, from Houston, TX. He released his first book of poetry, *Blurred Vision*, in 2011. Since then, he has released six poetry books and four novels. *A Swipe in the Wrong Direction* was inspired by his novel series that included *Fortune Cookie*, *No Cream in the Middle*, and *When the Cookie Crumbles*.

He enjoys providing healing, entertainment, and an occasional escape from reality through his writing. Carlos currently resides near Dallas, TX. Visit his website, peauxeticexpressions.com, to learn more. His next novel will detail a man who turns to illegal alternatives of earning an income to survive.

www.ingramcontent.com/pod-product-compliance
Lightning Source LLC
Chambersburg PA
CBHW071407290426
44108CB00014B/1721